Introduction

I0008476

In business, there are 2 key variables: Time and money. The birth of AI (artificial intelligence) has enabled individuals, business owners and entrepreneurs to achieve 3 key things:

- Save Time
- Save Money
- Reduce stress levels.

One of the largest costs in a business is payroll and think of all the tasks that AI could perform for you and deliver on time, within budget and without quibble. More importantly, AI can also help you in each of the 4 stages of the entrepreneurial journey to help you to identify, pursue and achieve your personal goals and objectives.

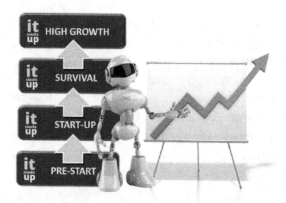

- **Pre-start:** Preparing, researching, and confirming that your business idea stacks up, makes sense, and will succeed.
- **Start-**up: Researching, planning & documenting your business model, customer journey, revenue streams and share your vision with stakeholders, shareholders & investors.
- **Survival:** Eliminating waste, reducing costs, and maximizing marketing and sales opportunities
- **High Growth:** AI can assist businesses poised for growth by assisting them to automate business processes and workflows

for maximum efficiency, scalability, and ROI.

Many people fail to turn their dream of starting a business, simply because they feel daunted by the sheer amount of work (and expense) that is required to get up and running and to sustain growth. Not anymore. By leveraging AI, they can automate key functions within their business, keep costs down whilst focusing on the priority tasks that need their attention:

- **Accounting and finance:** bookkeeping tasks, flag suspicious transactions, and predict financial outcomes based on trends and historical data.
- **Human resources:** hiring, onboarding and scheduling interviews, as well as providing analytics on employee engagement and performance.
- **Customer service:** providing customers with instant support and assistance, freeing up employees' time for more complex issues.
- **Data entry and analysis:** automating the collection, processing, and analysis of data, allowing for faster and more accurate insights.
- **Sales, Marketing, and advertising:** AI can analyze consumer behavior and preferences to create targeted campaigns and optimize ad placement.
- **Supply chain management:** AI can help automate inventory management, optimize shipping routes, and predict demand to ensure a streamlined supply chain.

More importantly by giving clear, specific, and concise commands and instructions (known as prompts) for the AI to perform the required tasks, you remain in control. Afterall, it's your business, you make the decisions, and you can delegate and automate the jobs you hate, don't have time for and simply don't want to do, allowing you to focus on key priorities in turning your idea into a reality. In fact, for the first time in history, starting and running a business couldn't be easier.

A dream with a date becomes a goal. A goal that is written down becomes a plan, a plan that is broken down into steps, tasks and prompts can be delegated and automated. More importantly, plans that are implemented, executed, and actioned, become a reality.

The purpose of this book is to encourage you to embrace AI to help you create and live your vision. It contains observations, reflections, and suggested prompts for leveraging AI on each stage of your entrepreneurial journey to fix, solve and overcome key challenges that you may face. If you're starting or growing your business, then I think you might just benefit from what I share in the following pages…if you **apply** what I share (or ask AI to do it for you.)

 When you see this symbol throughout the book. Pause & reflect. Make notes, Answer the Question or Complete the exercise. This will assist you.

Just reading and reflecting on the content will have little effect on the results you can and should be generating in your life, career, and business until you convert these "thoughts" into prompts and action by applying them and leveraging them via some of the resources I introduce you to, later. Sorry, but it's true. I can lead a horse to water, but I can't make it drink.

So, if you want to embrace, create, and live your vision, then ask yourself, what is the next job, task, or project that you want to automate?

Fraser J. Hay
March 2024

Copyright Notice

Thank you to Elsabe Smit – A true friend, teacher, and coach.
Thank you to ChatGPT for assisting me in saving me time, money &
stress.
Thank you to everyone else for the lessons you've taught me directly
or indirectly.
(They have been invaluable.)

PLEASE NOTE

Whilst I used ChatGPT to assist me in writing this book, you are
free to use the AI-powered assistant of your choice in your own
pursuits. When using your AI assistant, it will provide a draft for
your review &refinement. It is for educational purposes only and
can sometimes generate bad responses.

Therefore, any reliance on the provided information
is at your own risk and it should not be considered
as professional or legal advice. E&OE.

I recommend seeking advice from a mentor, business coach, lawyer
or other professional and not solely accept the response from
ChatGPT, Google Gemini & many other AI-powered tools available.

© Fraser J. Hay, 2024

All rights reserved. No part of this book may be reproduced in any
form or by any electronic or mechanical means including information
storage and retrieval system permission case of brief quotations in
articles or reviews – without the permission in writing from its
publisher.

Table of Contents

From Science Fiction to Daily Life

We all remember Arnold Schwarzenegger as the AI engineered cyborg, (model T1000) in the Hollywood terminator series of movies. But nowadays, AI (artificial intelligence) has become a ubiquitous part of our daily lives. From Fitbits to autonomous vehicles, AI is being used to improve our lives in countless ways. In this book, I'll share common entrepreneurial challenges, suggestions and potential questions, commands, instructions and prompts you can issue or ask your favourite AI-powered assistance to assist you in fixing, solving, or addressing some of your challenges in each of the 4 stages of the entrepreneurial journey.

One of the most well-known uses of AI is in personal assistants like Siri, Alexa, and Google Assistant. These virtual assistants use natural language processing and machine learning algorithms to understand our voice commands and respond with helpful information. They can answer questions, provide directions, play music, and even order food. Sometimes though, they can have difficulty with people's accents and dialects, and this can be frustrating.

AI is also used in healthcare, where it helps doctors diagnose diseases, analyze medical images, and develop personalized treatment plans. For example, an AI-powered tool called DeepMind is being used to analyze medical images and help doctors diagnose eye diseases more accurately.

Another common use of AI is in navigation apps like Google Maps and Waze. These apps use machine learning algorithms to analyze real-time traffic data and provide users with the best route to their destination. They can also alert drivers to accidents, road closures, and other hazards.

AI is also being used in the financial sector, where it's helping banks and financial institutions detect fraud, assess credit risk, and provide personalized financial advice. For example, JP Morgan has developed an AI-powered tool that can analyze legal documents and extract relevant information in a matter of seconds.

In the entertainment industry, AI is being used to create AI-generated music and art, as well as powering virtual reality experiences and video games. For example, a company called Amper Music has developed an AI-powered music composer that can generate original music based on a user's preferences. Just try tools like nightcafe or midjourney to create images in seconds. You can also use tools like Synthesia to create (almost human) avatars for your own promotional and instructional videos – in minutes.

AI is also being used in the field of education, where it's helping teachers personalise learning for students. For example, an AI-powered tool called DreamBox uses machine learning algorithms to analyze student data and provide personalized math instruction.

OpenAI is a research organization founded in December 2015 by a group of prominent technology entrepreneurs and investors, including Elon Musk, Sam Altman, Greg Brockman, Ilya Sutskever, Wojciech Zaremba, and John Schulman. The mission of OpenAI was to advance AI in a safe and beneficial way, ensuring that it serves humanity's best interests.

Over the years, OpenAI continued to make significant contributions to the field of AI, with breakthroughs in natural language processing, robotics, and computer vision. In 2019, the company released GPT-2's big brother, GPT-3, which stunned the world with its ability to generate highly coherent and human-like text, perform complex language tasks, and even write code.

OpenAI has emerged as one of the leading research organizations in the field of AI, with a mission to ensure that AI serves humanity's best interests. The company continues to push the boundaries of AI research and development, and its impact on the world is likely to be profound and far-reaching as it continues to stay ahead of major competitors like google.

Have you ever used Siri or Alexa to ask a question or perform a task such as playing a song from your favourite playlist? Or perhaps you've chatted with a customer service bot online? In all these cases, you're interacting with AI technology that has been trained to understand natural language.

But how does the AI system know what to do when you ask it a question or give it a command? That's where prompts come in.

Prompts are a way of giving AI systems a specific cue or instruction, so that they can generate a response that is relevant to your query. For example, if you ask Alexa

"What's the weather like today in Buckie, Scotland?"

Alexa will use a prompt to generate a response based on your location in Buckie and the current weather conditions.

Prompts can be simple, like the weather example above, or more complex, depending on the task at hand. They can be used to train machine learning models, to generate text for chatbots and virtual assistants, or to perform complex data analysis tasks.

To use prompts effectively, it's important to be clear and specific in your instructions. Instead of asking a general question like "What's the news?", try giving a more targeted prompt like "What are the top stories in tech today?" This will give the AI system more specific information to work with and increase the accuracy and relevance of the response.

Prompt Engineering in Your Business

As mentioned, Prompts are the important tools for communicating with AI systems in natural language. "Prompt Engineers" are now highly sought individuals and large salaries being offered to secure their expertise. By providing clear and specific cues, instructions, commands, and questions, you can help AI systems generate more accurate and relevant responses, whether you're using a virtual assistant, chatbot, or machine learning model.

Throughout my book I share prompts for you to tweak, customise and personalise to your current situation and the relevant stage you're at on your entrepreneurial journey.

Whether you want help to research, compare, list, write letters, emails, SOPs (standard operating procedures), conduct surveys or write adverts, video scripts or sales appointment scripts, the following 12 tips will help ensure you get the best possible results:

Use proper syntax: Make sure your sentences are properly structured with correct grammar and punctuation. This will help your AI-powered VA (virtual assistant) AI-powered better understand your intent and produce more coherent output.

Utilize parenthesis: Parentheses can be used to provide additional information or context to your AI-powered VA, which can help it generate more relevant and accurate responses.

Refine your prompts: Refine and edit your prompts before submitting them to your AI-powered VA to ensure they are clear and concise. The more specific and targeted your prompt, the better the output will be.

Avoid ambiguous language: Try to use clear and unambiguous language when asking questions or providing prompts to your AI-powered VA. This will help it understand your intent and produce more accurate responses.

Use the correct terminology: Be sure to use the correct terminology for the topic you are asking your AI-powered VA about. Using industry-specific language or jargon can help produce more accurate and relevant responses.

Be patient: your AI-powered VA may take some time to generate output, especially if it's processing a complex prompt. Be patient and wait for the output to be generated before making any assumptions.

Consider different perspectives: your AI-powered VA may provide output from different perspectives, so consider each response carefully and choose the one that is most relevant to your needs.

Verify the output: Always verify the output provided by your AI-powered VA for accuracy and relevancy. Don't assume that the output is correct without double-checking it.

Don't rely solely on your AI-powered VA: While it can be a useful tool, it's important not to rely solely on its output. Use your own judgement and knowledge to evaluate the output and make any necessary adjustments.

Provide feedback: Provide feedback to your AI-powered VA on its output to help it learn and improve over time. This can help produce more accurate and relevant responses in the future.

Continuously learn and improve: Continuously learn and improve your own writing and communication skills to help your AI-powered VA better understand your intent and produce more accurate output. The better your input, the better the output will be.

Apply the above hints, tips, and guidelines for each stage of your entrepreneurial journey.

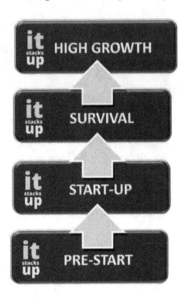

On my website, I take this one stage further, by helping you to start generating real confidence, progress, and results on each stage of your journey by following a very powerful, practical, and proven 4 step process.

it stacks **up**

PRE-START

Meaningful Work

Meaningful work is important when you're working for an employer. Meaningful work provides a sense of purpose and fulfillment in our lives, which is essential for our mental, emotional, and physical well-being. It is the feeling that what we are doing is valuable, useful, and contributing to something greater than ourselves often resulting in feeling valued, appreciated and in many cases, well rewarded or compensated for the knowledge, wisdom, talent, and skills you share and contribute to get the job in hand – done.

When we work for ourselves, meaningful work can be the driving force that motivates us to succeed. It is the reason we started our own business in the first place, and the satisfaction we get from doing something we believe in can be extremely rewarding. Working for ourselves also gives us the freedom to choose what we work on and how we approach it, which can lead to a deeper sense of purpose and satisfaction.

Similarly, when we work for someone else, meaningful work can be the key to job satisfaction and employee retention. Providing employees with work that is challenging, interesting, and purposeful can lead to higher levels of engagement, productivity, and loyalty. Conversely, many people leave jobs and seek employment elsewhere often not because of hating their boss, the commute or office politics, but because they lack fulfillment from their present job, role, or position.

So, whilst meaningful work is crucial whether you work for yourself or someone else, it provides a sense of purpose and fulfillment in our lives, which is essential for our mental and emotional well-being.

Each of the points below are split into 4 parts.

- **Challenge:** common issue or obstacle often faced by business owners
- **Fraserism:** a helpful hint, tip, quote, or suggestion to help

you in overcoming a challenge.

- **Potential Prompt:** a question, task, and prompt to ask your preferred ai-powered VA.
- **Benefit:** The potential benefit of researching, documenting, executing, automating, and refining a task, process, procedure, or workflow that addresses the underlying challenge.

Challenge: **Many people struggle to find work that aligns with their values and passions.**
Fraserism: Take the time to identify your core values and passions, and then seek out opportunities that align with them.
Potential Prompt: What steps can I take to identify my core values and passions?
Benefit: Finding work that aligns with your values and passions can lead to greater fulfillment and satisfaction.

Challenge: **Many people feel disconnected from the impact of their work**
Fraserism: Seek out opportunities to work on projects or in roles that have a clear and positive impact.
Potential Prompt: What are some ways I can find work that has a positive impact?
Benefit: Working on projects that have a positive impact can lead to a greater sense of purpose and fulfillment.

Challenge: **Many people feel stagnant or stuck in their current roles**
Fraserism: Seek out opportunities to learn new skills, take on new challenges, and push yourself out of your comfort zone.
Potential Prompt: What are some ways I can continue to learn and grow in my current role?
Benefit: Continuously learning and growing can lead to greater job satisfaction and a stronger sense of purpose.

Challenge: **Many people feel like they don't have control over their work**
Fraserism: Look for opportunities to take ownership of your work and make decisions that impact the outcome.

Potential Prompt: What steps can I take to gain more autonomy and control over my work?

Benefit: Having more autonomy and control can lead to greater job satisfaction and a sense of purpose.

Challenge: **Many people struggle to find a balance between work and their personal life.**

Fraserism: Set clear boundaries between work and personal time, and make sure to prioritize self-care and relaxation.

Potential Prompt: What are some ways I can improve my work-life balance?

Benefit: Having a good work-life balance can lead to greater overall happiness and fulfillment.

Challenge: **Many people feel like their work is not recognized or valued by their employer.**

Fraserism: Look for opportunities to showcase your work and communicate its value to others.

Potential Prompt: What are some ways I can ensure that my work is recognized and valued by others?

Benefit: Feeling recognized and valued can lead to greater job satisfaction and motivation.

Challenge: **Many people struggle with difficult colleagues or supervisors**

Fraserism: Work on building positive relationships with your colleagues and supervisor and communicate openly and honestly.

Potential Prompt: What are some ways I can improve my relationships with my colleagues and supervisor?

Benefit: Having good relationships with colleagues and a supportive supervisor can lead to greater job satisfaction and a sense of purpose.

Challenge: **You feel like you're lacking focus and direction in your current role.**

Fraserism: Try setting SMART (Specific, Measurable, Achievable, Relevant, Time-bound) goals to help you clarify your objectives and stay on track.

Prompt: "How can I set specific and achievable goals to improve my focus and direction at work?"

Benefit: Setting SMART goals can help you gain a sense of direction, motivation, and focus, leading to increased productivity and job satisfaction.

The challenge: **You struggle to manage your workload and feel constantly stressed.**
Fraserism: Implement time-management techniques, such as prioritizing tasks, delegating responsibilities, and setting boundaries.
Prompt: "What time-management techniques can I implement to reduce stress and improve productivity?"
Benefit: Effective time-management can reduce stress, improve productivity, and help you achieve a better work-life balance.

The challenge: **You feel like you're not fulfilling your life purpose in your current role.**
Fraserism: Explore new career opportunities or consider volunteering outside of work to find fulfillment.
Prompt: "What steps can I take to explore new career opportunities or find fulfillment outside of work?"
Benefit: Finding fulfillment in your career or personal life can lead to greater happiness and a sense of purpose.

The challenge: **You find your work monotonous and unfulfilling.**
Fraserism: Try to find ways to make your work more engaging, such as taking on new responsibilities or learning new skills.
Prompt: "How can I make my work more engaging and fulfilling?"
Benefit: Making your work more engaging and fulfilling can lead to increased job satisfaction and motivation.

The challenge: **You struggle to keep up with rising costs and debt.**
Fraserism: Create a budget and plan to pay off debt.
Prompt: "How can I create a budget and pay off debt to improve my financial stability?"
Benefit: Managing your finances can reduce stress and improve your overall quality of life.

The challenge: **You struggle to manage your time effectively and meet deadlines.**
Fraserism: Use tools such as a calendar or project management

software to help you manage your time and meet deadlines.

Prompt: "What tools can I use to improve my time-management skills and meet deadlines?"

Benefit: Improving your time-management skills can reduce stress and improve your productivity.

The challenge: **You're ready for a new challenge and positive change in your career.**

Fraserism: Consider exploring new career opportunities or taking on new responsibilities in your current role.

Prompt: "Which websites allow me to set email alerts on vacancies matching my skills?"

Benefit: Taking on new challenges can help you grow and develop in your career, leading to increased job satisfaction and motivation.

The challenge: **You feel undervalued and underpaid in your current role.**

Fraserism: Consider negotiating a salary increase or seeking new career opportunities.

Prompt: "What steps can I take to negotiate a salary increase or explore new career opportunities?"

Benefit: Negotiating a fair salary or finding a new job can improve your financial stability.

 Q. Are you Enjoying Meaningful Work? If not, you could research new job opportunities. Do you use AI to help you gain clarity, vision, and purpose to embrace, create and live your vision?

1. Yes. All done, planned, documented & ready for the next stage.

2. On the case. Working towards it, documenting it.

3. Oops. No, not yet completed (or started).

4. This is all too overwhelming. I Need help with this – fast.

Kodak was a global leader in the photography industry, with a peak revenue of $19.6 billion in 1996. However, Kodak was slow to embrace digital photography, despite inventing the first digital camera in 1975.

This allowed competitors like Canon and Nikon to gain an advantage, and Kodak eventually filed for bankruptcy in 2012.

Ensure you embrace technology & stay ahead of your competitors to create & live your vision.

Get AI-powered help to save time, money & stress to do the jobs you hate, don't have time for, or simply don't want to do.

Reduce costs, improve efficiency & ROI to achieve your goals & objectives. It's your business. you're in control.
You make the decisions.
You decide what you want to achieve next.

At a crossroads

Being at a crossroads and facing the decision of whether to get another job or start your own business can be a daunting and overwhelming experience. It is a pivotal moment in one's life that requires careful consideration and reflection.

I remember the day I made the decision to leave a good job as the marketing manager in a cosmetics company to start my own business, but I wasn't prepared for what happened next, after I made my decision. I share more about that in my TEDx talk – HERE.

t's normal to feel conflicted about the idea of starting your own business versus working for someone else. The security of a steady paycheck can be appealing, but the potential rewards of entrepreneurship can be tempting. You may have doubts about your abilities to run a successful business and feel uncertain about taking risks.

It's important to acknowledge these mixed emotions and consider the pros and cons of each option before deciding. Evaluating your personal goals, values, and financial situation can also help guide your choice.

One common concern for entrepreneurs is the workload and the tasks that they may not have the skills or desire to complete. This is where AI can provide a helpful solution in the form of "Skillutions." These are packaged automated solutions that can complete tasks and instructions efficiently and accurately, saving time, money, and stress. By giving specific prompts to AI, you can delegate tasks and focus on what you do best.

Working for yourself involves working long hours, making difficult and hard decisions and many people worry about finding the time to do the jobs they don't want to do, hate doing or simply lack the skills to do them. That's where AI (artificial intelligence) can provide **"Skillutions;"** a packaged solution that can save you time, money, and stress by acting efficiently, and diligently to complete the jobs, tasks, and instructions that you share via clear and specific "prompts" that command it to provide the Skillution you want.

Having said that, using AI can often yield some surprising and life changing results. Here are a few suggestions to help you find, create, or pursue meaningful work through self-employment or in starting your own business.

Each of the points below are split into 4 parts.

- **Challenge:** common issue or obstacle often faced by business owners
- **Fraserism:** a helpful hint, tip, quote, or suggestion to help you in overcoming a challenge.
- **Potential Prompt:** a question, task, and prompt to ask your preferred ai-powered VA.
- **Benefit:** The potential benefit of researching, documenting, executing, automating, and refining a task, process, procedure, or workflow that addresses the underlying challenge.

Challenge: **Overwhelmed by the process of becoming self-employed**

Fraserism: Break down the process into smaller steps and create a plan.

Potential Prompt: "How can I simplify the process of becoming self-employed?"

Benefit: By breaking down the process into smaller steps, you can manage each task more easily and feel less overwhelmed. You will also have a clear plan of action, which will help you feel more confident and motivated.

Challenge: **Struggling to justify experience, skills, or knowledge to clients or customers.**

Fraserism: Create a portfolio or case studies to showcase your expertise.

Potential Prompt: "How can I show potential clients that I have the skills and experience they need?"

Benefit: By creating a portfolio or case studies, you can provide concrete examples of your work and demonstrate your capabilities. This will help potential clients or customers feel more confident in your abilities and increase the likelihood of them hiring or purchasing from you.

Challenge: **Uncertainty around starting a business due to lack of invention or start-up capital.**

Fraserism: Focus on identifying a problem that needs solving and creating a solution.

Potential Prompt: "How can I start a business without a unique invention or much start-up capital?"

Benefit: By focusing on solving a problem, you can create a business that provides value to customers or clients, even if you don't have a unique invention or a lot of start-up capital. This approach can help you create a business that is more likely to succeed in the long term.

Challenge: **Uncertainty around how to create a business plan.**

Fraserism: Investigate online resources and templates to guide you in creating a plan.

Potential Prompt: "What are the key elements that should be included in a business plan?"

Benefit: By using online resources and templates, you can gain a better understanding of what should be included in a business plan and create a plan that is more likely to be successful. This can help you secure funding or investment and provide a roadmap for your business.

Challenge: **Uncertainty around finding or generating leads for your business.**
Fraserism: Utilize social media and networking to connect with potential clients or customers.
Potential Prompt: "How can I find or generate leads for my business?"
Benefit: By utilizing social media and networking or by exploring what's available on itstacksup.com, you can connect with potential clients or customers and generate leads for your business. This approach can help you build relationships and increase the likelihood of securing business.

Challenge: **Concerns about not receiving support from family or appearing foolish.**
Fraserism: Seek out a mentor or join a community of like-minded individuals for support.
Potential Prompt: "How can I find support as I start my business?"
Benefit: By finding a mentor or joining a community, you can receive support and guidance from others who have been in your shoes. This can help you stay motivated, overcome challenges, and reduce the fear of failure.

Challenge: **Lack of confidence in sales and conversion skills.**
Fraserism: Practice sales techniques and consider taking courses or workshops.
Potential Prompt: "How can I improve my sales and conversion skills?"
Benefit: By practicing sales techniques and taking courses or workshops, you can improve your sales and conversion skills and increase the likelihood of closing deals. This can help you grow your business and increase revenue.

Challenge: **Concerns around protecting your idea.**
Fraserism: Research and utilize legal resources to protect your intellectual property.

Potential Prompt: "How can I protect my business idea?"
Benefit: By utilizing legal resources to protect your intellectual property, you can safeguard your business idea and prevent others from stealing it. This can help you feel more secure and increase the likelihood of long-term success.

Challenge: **Uncertainty about idea viability.**
Fraserism: Conduct market research and validate the potential of your idea before investing time and resources.
Potential Prompt: "What steps can I take to validate the viability of my business idea?"
Benefit: Conducting market research and validating your idea can help you identify potential challenges and opportunities, leading to a more informed decision about pursuing self-employment.

Challenge: **Anxiety about salary.**
Fraserism: Conduct a financial analysis to determine whether you can sustain your lifestyle on a potentially fluctuating income.
Potential Prompt: "How can I determine whether I can sustain my lifestyle on potentially fluctuating income?"
Benefit: Conducting a financial analysis can help you determine whether self-employment is financially feasible, and if not, it can help you identify areas where you can reduce your expenses.

Challenge: **Concerns about pricing.**
Fraserism: Research industry standards and determine the value of your products or services to set appropriate prices.
Potential Prompt: "How can I set appropriate prices for my products or services?"
Benefit: Researching industry standards and setting appropriate prices can help you attract customers and generate revenue that aligns with the value of your offerings.

Challenge: **Lack of confidence in selling skills.**
Fraserism: Invest in sales and marketing training to improve your skills and confidence.
Potential Prompt: "How can I improve my selling skills and confidence?"
Benefit: Improving your selling skills and confidence can help you

generate more leads, close more sales, and grow your business.

Challenge: **Anxiety about generating traffic and sales.**
Fraserism: Develop a strategic marketing plan to attract your target audience and convert them into customers.
Potential Prompt: "How can I develop a strategic marketing plan to generate traffic and sales?"
Benefit: Developing a strategic marketing plan can help you effectively reach your target audience, increase brand awareness, and generate more leads and sales.

Challenge: **Uncertainty about competition.**
Fraserism: Conduct a competitive analysis to identify your strengths and weaknesses relative to your competitors.
Potential Prompt: "How can I conduct a competitive analysis to identify my strengths and weaknesses relative to my competitors?"
Benefit: Conducting a competitive analysis can help you identify areas where you can differentiate yourself from your competitors and develop a competitive advantage.

Challenge: **High personal overheads.**
Fraserism: Develop a budget and identify areas where you can reduce expenses to lower your personal overheads.
Potential Prompt: "How can I develop a budget and reduce my personal overheads?"
Benefit: Developing a budget and reducing your personal overheads can help you free up funds to invest in your business and reduce financial stress.

Challenge: **Anxiety about premises.**
Fraserism: Research and weigh the pros and cons of different premises options to determine the best fit for your business.
Potential Prompt: "How can I determine the best premises option for my business?"
Benefit: Identifying the best premises option for your business can help you create a productive and efficient workspace that supports your business goals.

Challenge: **Difficulty finding trustworthy help.**

Fraserism: Develop a thorough hiring process that includes background checks and reference checks to ensure you hire trustworthy employees.

Potential Prompt: "How can I develop a hiring process to ensure I hire trustworthy employees?"

Benefit: Developing a thorough hiring process can help you build a reliable and trustworthy team that supports your business growth.

Challenge: **Website optimization.**

Fraserism: Work with a web developer or invest in learning website optimization techniques to maximize the effectiveness of your website.

Potential Prompt: "How can I optimize my website to maximize its effectiveness?"

Benefit: Optimizing your website can help you attract more traffic, generate more leads, and increase conversions, leading to increased revenue and business growth.

Q. Are you at a crossroads? Considering self-employment or starting a business? Do you use AI to help you gain clarity, vision, and purpose to embrace, create and live your vision?

1. Yes. All done, planned, documented & ready for the next stage.

2. On the case. Working towards it, documenting it.

3. Oops. No, not yet completed (or started).

4. This is all too overwhelming. I Need help with this – fast.

Your Life Purpose

Having a clear sense of life purpose is like having a compass that guides you towards your desired destination. Just like a compass helps hikers navigate through uncharted territory, a life purpose helps individuals navigate through life's twists and turns, providing direction and meaning to their existence or as I like to say, it's being "on point, on form and on fire."

When you have a life purpose, you can focus your energy and resources on what truly matters to you and avoid getting sidetracked by distractions and obstacles. It's like having a road map that helps you stay on course towards your goals, even during tough times when motivation is low.

In fact, having a life purpose can help you find motivation during challenging times, as it gives you a reason to keep going, even when things get tough. It can also help you make better decisions by aligning your choices with your values and beliefs.

For me, the meaning of life is like unwrapping a present to discover what's inside. Each person has a unique gift to share with the world, and the purpose of life is to unwrap that gift and share it with others. And sometimes, life presents us with unexpected opportunities and challenges that help us discover new gifts and talents.

Ultimately, having a life purpose can lead to a sense of fulfillment and satisfaction, as you work towards achieving your personal vision of success. Whether that means starting your own business or pursuing a different career path, it's important to evaluate your strengths, weaknesses, and financial resources before making any major decisions.

If you're unsure about your life purpose, here are some tips to help you discover it. You can reflect on your passions, interests, and values, and think about how you can use them to make a positive impact on the world. And if you need some extra guidance, you can always ask AI to assist you in discovering your purpose and reaching your full potential. Each of the points below are split into 4 parts.

- **Challenge:** common issue or obstacle often faced by business owners
- **Fraserism:** a helpful hint, tip, quote, or suggestion to help you in overcoming a challenge.
- **Potential Prompt:** a question, task, and prompt to ask your preferred ai-powered VA.
- **Benefit:** The potential benefit of researching, documenting, executing, automating, and refining a task, process, procedure, or workflow that addresses the underlying challenge.

Challenge: **You are not clear on your life purpose.**
Suggestion:Start by exploring your passions and values. Ask yourself what makes you happy and fulfilled. Try new things and take note of what brings you joy and purpose. Pay attention to what comes naturally to you and what you excel in. Seek guidance from a mentor or coach if needed.
Potential Prompt: What steps can I take to discover my passions and values?
Benefit: By exploring your passions and values, you can gain even more clarity on your life purpose and what brings you meaning and fulfillment. In my webinars, workshops and coaching, I often ask 3 key questions:

- What are you good at?
- What do you enjoy doing?
- If you had no change of failure, what would you do next with your life?

Challenge: **You do not know how to get clarity on your life purpose.**
Suggestion:Practice self-reflection and introspection. Meditate, journal, and ask yourself meaningful questions such as "What is my unique purpose in life?" or "What impact do I want to make on the

world?". Seek feedback from trusted friends and family who know you well and can offer an outside perspective.

Potential Prompt: How can I incorporate self-reflection into my daily routine?

Benefit: By regularly practicing self-reflection, you can gain insights and clarity on your life purpose.

Challenge: **You are not on your path of discovering your life purpose.**

Suggestion:Take action towards your passions and goals. Set achievable goals and create a plan of action to get there. Take risks and embrace failure as a learning opportunity. Surround yourself with positive and supportive people who encourage and inspire you.

Potential Prompt: What small steps can I take today towards my goals?

Benefit: By taking action towards your goals, you can gain momentum and build confidence in yourself and your ability to discover your life purpose.

Challenge: **You are not living your life purpose.**

Suggestion:Evaluate your current life and make necessary changes to align with your purpose. Prioritize your time and energy towards activities that align with your values and bring you joy. Be open to new opportunities and experiences that may lead you closer to your purpose.

Potential Prompt: What changes do I need to make in my life to align with my purpose?

Benefit: By aligning your life with your purpose, you can experience greater fulfillment and meaning in your daily life.

Challenge: **You do not know what you need to accomplish your life purpose.**

Suggestion:Seek guidance from a mentor or coach who can offer insight and support. Break down your goals into manageable steps and create a plan of action. Embrace failure as a learning opportunity and adjust your plan accordingly.

Potential Prompt: Who can I reach out to for guidance and support in achieving my goals?

Benefit: By seeking guidance and creating a plan of action, you can gain clarity and direction towards achieving your life purpose.

Challenge: **You are not happy with the results you are achieving at the moment.**
Suggestion:Reevaluate your goals and priorities. Practice gratitude and focus on the positives in your life. Embrace a growth mindset and view setbacks as opportunities for learning and growth.
Potential Prompt: How can I practice gratitude and focus on the positives in my life?
Benefit: By practicing gratitude and embracing a growth mindset, you can shift your perspective towards a more positive and fulfilling life.

Challenge: **You do not know what you need to change in order to achieve your life purpose.**
Suggestion:Evaluate your current habits and behaviors. Identify what is holding you back and make necessary changes to align with your purpose. Seek feedback from trusted friends and family who can offer an outside perspective.
Potential Prompt: What habits and behaviors do I need to change in order to align with my purpose?
Benefit: By identifying and making necessary changes, you can create a clear path towards achieving your life purpose.

Challenge: **Lack of motivation and direction in life.**
Suggestion:Take time to reflect on your values, interests, and passions to gain clarity on your life purpose.
Potential Prompt: What are your top values, interests, and passions in life? How do they align with your current lifestyle and goals?
Benefit: By gaining a deeper understanding of your values, interests, and passions, you can create a life plan that aligns with your purpose and provides direction and motivation.

Challenge: **Feeling lost or unsure of what steps to take next.**
Suggestion:Seek guidance and support from a mentor or coach who can help you create a clear action plan for achieving your life purpose.

Potential Prompt: What are your biggest challenges in achieving your life purpose? How can a mentor or coach help you overcome these challenges and achieve your goals?

Benefit: By working with a mentor or coach, you can gain valuable insights and strategies for achieving your life purpose, and receive support and accountability along the way.

Challenge: **Difficulty in identifying personal strengths and talents.**

Suggestion:Take a strengths assessment or seek feedback from trusted friends or colleagues to gain insight into your unique talents and strengths.

Potential Prompt: What feedback have you received from others about your strengths and talents? What strengths assessment tools have you used in the past?

Benefit: By identifying your unique strengths and talents, you can leverage them to achieve your life purpose and increase your overall satisfaction and success.

Challenge: **Fear or self-doubt holding you back from pursuing your life purpose.**

Suggestion:Practice self-compassion and positive self-talk, and focus on small, achievable goals to build confidence and overcome fear.

Potential Prompt: What self-doubts or fears do you have around pursuing your life purpose? How can you practice self-compassion and positive self-talk to overcome these obstacles?

Benefit: By cultivating self-compassion and confidence, you can overcome fear and self-doubt and take bold steps towards achieving your life purpose.

Challenge: **Feeling overwhelmed or stressed by daily life.**

Suggestion:Practice mindfulness, meditation, or other stress-reducing activities to manage stress and stay focused on your life purpose.

Potential Prompt: What stress-reducing activities have you tried in the past? How have they helped you manage stress and stay focused on your goals?

Benefit: By reducing stress and cultivating mindfulness, you can stay focused on your life purpose and make progress towards your goals with greater ease and clarity.

Challenge: **Lack of clarity or direction in career or job.**
Suggestion:Explore career or job options that align with your values, interests, and strengths, and seek guidance from a career counselor or coach.
Potential Prompt: What are your top career or job-related values, interests, and strengths? How can you explore options that align with these factors?
Benefit: By finding a career or job that aligns with your purpose and strengths, you can experience greater fulfillment and success in your professional life.

Challenge: **Difficulty in staying motivated or committed to long-term goals.**
Suggestion:Break down long-term goals into smaller, achievable steps, and celebrate each milestone along the way.
Potential Prompt: What long-term goals do you have for achieving your life purpose? How can you break these goals down into smaller, achievable steps?
Benefit: By setting achievable goals and celebrating each milestone, you can stay on point, on form and on fire.

Q. Are you on point, on form and on fire? Do you know and are you living your life purpose? Do you use AI to help you gain clarity, vision, and purpose to embrace, create and live your vision?

1. Yes. All done, I am on point, on form and on fire.
2. On the case. Working towards it, documenting it.
3. Oops. No, not yet completed (or started).
4. This is all too overwhelming. I Need help with this – fast.

Your Fears

For many, starting a business can feel like stepping into a vast and uncharted territory. With so much to consider, it's not surprising that entrepreneurs may experience a range of fears and concerns as they embark on their journey.

One common area of concern is legal compliance. Entrepreneurs often feel overwhelmed by the complex regulations surrounding their industry, unsure of how to navigate the legal landscape, and worried about protecting their intellectual property. It's important to seek out expert advice and guidance to ensure you're operating within the bounds of the law.

Technical expertise is another area that can cause anxiety for entrepreneurs. With new technologies emerging all the time, it can be challenging to stay up-to-date and ensure data privacy and security. However, there are resources available to help entrepreneurs develop and maintain their technical skills, such as online courses and tutorials.

Financial concerns are also a common worry for entrepreneurs. Starting a business often requires a significant investment of capital, and entrepreneurs may struggle to secure funding, manage cash flow, and navigate economic downturns. Developing a solid financial plan and seeking out funding opportunities can help alleviate some of these concerns.

Emotional concerns, such as stress and work-life balance, can also weigh heavily on entrepreneurs. Starting a business can be an isolating experience, but building a support network of mentors, peers, and family members can provide much-needed emotional support and guidance.

Finally, marketing and sales can be a daunting area for many entrepreneurs. However, there are many resources available to help entrepreneurs identify their target audience, develop effective marketing strategies, and create a compelling brand. It's important to invest time and energy in building a strong marketing and sales plan to help your business succeed.

Overall, while starting a business can be challenging and complex, addressing your fears and seeking support can help entrepreneurs overcome obstacles and build a successful business.

Each of the points below are split into 4 parts.

- **Challenge:** common issue or obstacle often faced by business owners
- **Fraserism:** a helpful hint, tip, quote, or suggestion to help you in overcoming a challenge.
- **Potential Prompt:** a question, task, and prompt to ask your preferred ai-powered VA.
- **Benefit:** The potential benefit of researching, documenting, executing, automating, and refining a task, process, procedure, or workflow that addresses the underlying challenge.

Challenge: **Feeling overwhelmed about what's involved in becoming self-employed.**
Fraserism: Break down the process of becoming self-employed into smaller, manageable tasks and prioritize them based on their importance. Create a timeline and set achievable goals for each task.
Potential Prompt: "Can you give me some guidance on how to break down the process of becoming self-employed into smaller, manageable tasks?"
Benefit: By breaking down the process, it will be easier to manage and will help you stay focused on achieving your goals.

Challenge: **Struggling to find where to start in becoming self-employed.**
Fraserism: Do research on the industry you want to enter, network with professionals in that field, and seek advice from those who have experience in self-employment.
Potential Prompt: "What steps can I take to research the industry I

want to enter and network with professionals in that field?"

Benefit: By doing research and seeking advice, you will gain a better understanding of the industry and the necessary steps to become self-employed.

Challenge: **Still weighing up the pros and cons of becoming self-employed.**

Fraserism: Make a list of the pros and cons of becoming self-employed and evaluate them based on your personal goals and values. Seek advice from those who have experience in self-employment.

Potential Prompt: "How can I evaluate the pros and cons of becoming self-employed based on my personal goals and values?"

Benefit: By evaluating the pros and cons, you will gain a better understanding of whether self-employment aligns with your personal goals and values.

Challenge: **Struggling to justify the experience, skills, and knowledge you have.**

Fraserism: Create a portfolio of your work and accomplishments, and seek feedback from others in your industry. Develop a clear and concise elevator pitch to showcase your skills and experience to potential clients or investors.

Potential Prompt: "How can I create a portfolio of my work and accomplishments and develop an effective elevator pitch?"

Benefit: By creating a portfolio and elevator pitch, you will be able to showcase your skills and experience effectively to potential clients or investors.

Challenge: **Unsure about working for yourself because you haven't invented anything.**

Fraserism: Focus on your unique skills and experience, and identify how they can be applied to a specific industry or market. Seek advice from others who have experience in that industry or market.

Potential Prompt: "How can I identify how my unique skills and experience can be applied to a specific industry or market?"

Benefit: By focusing on your unique skills and experience, you can identify how to position yourself in a specific industry or market and stand out from competitors.

Challenge: **Frustrated because you don't have much (or any) start-up capital.**

Fraserism: Identify low-cost or free resources and tools to help you start your business, such as free business plan templates, free marketing tools, or low-cost business loans. Consider bootstrapping your business to keep costs low.

Potential Prompt: "What are some low-cost or free resources and tools I can use to start my business?"

Benefit: By identifying low-cost or free resources and tools, you can save money and still effectively start your business.

Challenge: **Anxious because you haven't protected your idea yet.**

Fraserism: Research and understand the intellectual property laws in your country or region, and seek advice from a lawyer specializing in intellectual property. Consider filing for a patent or trademark to protect your idea.

Potential Prompt: "How can I protect my idea through patents or trademarks and what are the steps involved?"

Benefit: By protecting your idea, you can prevent others from copying or stealing it and retain ownership of your intellectual property.

Challenge: **Uncertainty about the viability of the business idea.**

My Fraserism: Conduct market research and gather feedback from potential customers to validate the idea's feasibility.

Potential Prompt: How can I determine if my business idea is viable in the market?

Benefit: The benefit of conducting market research is that it provides valuable insights into the target audience's needs, preferences, and pain points, which can be used to refine the business idea and increase the chances of success.

Challenge: **Anxiety about earning a salary from the business.**

My Fraserism: Develop a realistic financial plan that outlines the business's revenue streams, expenses, and projected profits.

Potential Prompt: How can I ensure that my business generates enough revenue to cover my salary?

Benefit: A realistic financial plan provides a clear understanding of the business's financial health, allowing entrepreneurs to make informed decisions that maximize profits and minimize risks.

Challenge: **Worries about pricing and customer willingness to pay.**
My Fraserism: Conduct market research to determine the average prices for similar products or services and analyze customer behavior to identify the factors that influence their willingness to pay.
Potential Prompt: How can I determine the right price for my products/services?
Benefit: Setting the right prices can increase profitability, attract more customers, and establish the business as a competitive player in the market.

Challenge: **Lack of confidence in selling skills.**
My Fraserism: Practice and develop persuasive communication skills to effectively sell the business's products or services.
Potential Prompt: How can I improve my sales skills and confidence?
Benefit: Effective selling skills can increase revenue, attract more customers, and build a loyal customer base.

Challenge: **Uncertainty about generating website traffic and leads.**
My Fraserism: Develop a comprehensive digital marketing plan that includes SEO, social media, content marketing, email marketing, and paid advertising.
Potential Prompt: How can I generate more traffic and sales to my website?
Benefit: A comprehensive digital marketing plan can increase website traffic, improve lead generation, and boost sales and revenue.

Challenge: **Difficulty finding trustworthy employees.**
My Fraserism: Develop a rigorous recruitment process that includes thorough background checks, reference checks, and skills assessment.
Potential Prompt: How can I ensure that I hire trustworthy employees for my business?
Benefit: A rigorous recruitment process can minimize the risk of hiring untrustworthy employees, improve team performance, and enhance the business's reputation.

Q. Are you on point, on form and on fire? Do you know and are you living your life purpose? Do you use AI to help you gain clarity, vision, and purpose to embrace, create and live your vision?

1. Yes. All done, I am on point, on form and on fire.
2. On the case. Working towards it, documenting it.
3. Oops. No, not yet completed (or started).
4. This is all too overwhelming. I Need help with this – fast.

Blockbuster was a leading video rental chain with over 9,000 stores at its peak in 2004. However, Blockbuster failed to embrace online streaming and rental services like Netflix, which eventually led to their demise. Blockbuster filed for bankruptcy in 2010 and closed all its remaining stores in 2013. Ensure you embrace technology & stay ahead of your competitors to create & live your vision.

Get AI-powered help to save time, money & stress to do the jobs you hate, don't have time for, or simply don't want to do.

Reduce costs, improve efficiency & ROI to achieve your goals & objectives. It's your business. you're in control. You make the decisions.

You decide what you want to achieve next.

Reasons For Starting a Business

Starting a business can be an exhilarating adventure, but it's crucial to have strong, personal reasons for doing so. Your reasons are the fuel that will keep your business moving forward, just like a car needs gas to keep going. But what are good reasons for starting a business?

Your reasons for starting a business should come from a place of authenticity and personal drive. They should be rooted in your values, passions, and goals. You're motivated by a desire for financial independence or a passion for a particular product or service. You have a specific problem that you want to solve or a legacy that you want to leave behind. The key is to be honest with yourself about what drives you and what you want to achieve.

However, it's not enough to simply have reasons; they also need to be realistic and well thought-out. Starting a business is a significant commitment, and you want to ensure that you have a solid foundation to build upon. This means doing research to confirm that there is a viable market for your business idea and a clear path to success.

Once you've established your reasons for starting a business, it's essential to remain focused and motivated. There will be obstacles to overcome, but if you have a clear and compelling purpose, you'll be more likely to push through difficult times and stay true to your vision.

When sharing your reasons with others, it's vital to communicate with them effectively. AI can be a useful tool in this regard. By analyzing your message and story, AI can help ensure that your message is coming across the way you intended. Furthermore, AI can assist in identifying any gaps or inconsistencies in your reasoning and prompt you to clarify your thoughts.

So, having solid reasons for starting a business is crucial for long-term success and fulfillment. Take the time to establish your reasons and ensure they align with your values and goals. Utilise AI to help you communicate your message and "story" effectively and attract the right people to support your vision. Remember, your reasons are the fuel that will keep your business running for the long haul.

Each of the points below are split into 4 parts.

- **Challenge:** common issue or obstacle often faced by business owners
- **Fraserism:** a helpful hint, tip, quote, or suggestion to help you in overcoming a challenge.
- **Potential Prompt:** a question, task, and prompt to ask your preferred ai-powered VA.
- **Benefit:** The potential benefit of researching, documenting, executing, automating, and refining a task, process, procedure, or workflow that addresses the underlying challenge.

Challenge: **Feeling undervalued or unappreciated in your current job.**
Fraserism: Ask yourself if starting a business would allow you to feel more valued and appreciated.
Potential Prompt: "Would starting a business give me the opportunity to feel more valued and appreciated for my skills and contributions?"
Benefit: By considering the potential benefits of starting a business, you may gain a new perspective on your current situation and feel more empowered to take action.

Challenge: **Hating your job, boss, or commuting to work.**
Fraserism: Explore how starting a business could improve your overall job satisfaction.
Potential Prompt: "How would starting a business improve my daily work experience and overall job satisfaction?"
Benefit: By focusing on the potential benefits of starting a business, you may feel more motivated to take action and create a more fulfilling career path for yourself.

Challenge: **Wanting to work for yourself and be your own boss.**
Fraserism: Consider the benefits of being self-employed and the

potential for personal growth and fulfillment.

Potential Prompt: "What are the personal benefits of being my own boss and working for myself?"

Benefit: By identifying the potential personal benefits of starting a business, you may feel more motivated to pursue your goals and take control of your career.

Challenge: **Wanting to take control of your life.**

Fraserism: Consider how starting a business could give you greater control over your time, finances, and overall quality of life.

Potential Prompt: "How would starting a business give me greater control over my time, finances, and overall quality of life?"

Benefit: By focusing on the potential benefits of starting a business, you may feel more empowered to take control of your life and pursue your goals.

Challenge: **Wanting to live your "life purpose."**

Fraserism: Consider how starting a business could help you align your career with your personal values and passions and in wanting to get on point, on form and on fire.

Potential Prompt: "How could starting a business help me align my career with my personal values and passions?"

Benefit: By focusing on the potential benefits of starting a business, you may gain greater clarity on your personal goals and feel more motivated to pursue them.

Challenge: **Yearning for a more rewarding and fulfilling job, role, career, or "life."**

Fraserism: Consider how starting a business could provide greater fulfillment and meaning in your career and life.

Potential Prompt: "How could starting a business provide greater fulfillment and meaning in my career and life?"

Benefit: By focusing on the potential benefits of starting a business, you may feel more motivated to pursue a career path that aligns with your personal goals and values.

Challenge: **Considering working for yourself for 3 months or longer.**

Fraserism: Consider the potential benefits and challenges of starting a business and weigh the risks and rewards.

Potential Prompt: "What are the potential benefits and challenges of starting a business and how do they compare to my current situation?"

Benefit: By considering the potential benefits and challenges of starting a business, you can make a more informed decision about whether it's the right choice for you.

Challenge: **Having a hobby or passion you'd like to turn into a business.**

Fraserism: Explore how you can monetize your passion and turn it into a profitable business.

Potential Prompt: "How can I monetize my hobby or passion and turn it into a profitable business?"

Benefit: By exploring the potential business opportunities related to your hobby or passion, you may find a new career path that aligns with your interests and goals.

Challenge: **Lack of fair compensation for your time and effort.**

Fraserism: Starting a business does not guarantee that you will be fairly compensated for your time and effort. In fact, it may take some time for your business to generate a profit. However, if you can build a successful business, it can provide you with the potential to earn more than you would in a regular job.

Potential Prompt: "Do you want to start a business to be fairly compensated for your time and effort?"

Benefit: This prompt can help you assess your motivations for starting a business and determine whether your expectations are realistic.

Challenge: **Lack of confidence in your ability to offer your skills for a fee.**

Fraserism: Starting a business requires confidence in your abilities and the value that you can provide to customers. If you are unsure of your skills or doubt your ability to offer them for a fee, it may be worth taking the time to build your confidence and skills before starting a business.

Potential Prompt: "Do you feel confident in offering your skills, knowledge or talent for a fee?"

Benefit: This prompt can help you assess your readiness to start a business and identify any areas where you may need to improve your skills or confidence.

Challenge: **Uncertainty around whether people will want to buy your product or service.**
Fraserism: It can be difficult to determine whether people will want to buy your product or service before launching your business. However, market research and testing can help you to determine the demand for your product or service and identify potential customers.
Potential Prompt: "Do you think people will pay the fees you want to charge working for yourself?"
Benefit: This prompt can help you assess the viability of your business idea and identify any potential challenges around pricing.

Challenge: **Lack of knowledge or experience in bookkeeping and financial management.**
Fraserism: Starting a business requires financial management skills, such as bookkeeping and budgeting. If you lack experience in these areas, it may be worth investing in training or hiring a professional to manage your finances.
Potential Prompt: "Would you consider self-employment if someone else took care of all the bookkeeping?"
Benefit: This prompt can help you identify potential solutions for any gaps in your skills or knowledge and can help you assess whether you are willing to invest in resources such as hiring a professional to support your business.

Challenge: **Lack of consistent sales or income.**
Fraserism: Starting a business does not guarantee consistent sales or income, especially in the early stages. However, developing a strong marketing and sales strategy can help you to increase sales and build a steady customer base.
Potential Prompt: "Would you consider working for yourself if you knew sales would come in every month?"
Benefit: This prompt can help you assess the potential risks and rewards of starting a business and can help you to identify any areas where you may need to improve your sales and marketing efforts.

Q. Do you have good reasons for starting a business or are just reacting to what life presents to you? Sometimes, we need good reasons for wanting to start a business and not just excuses. Do you use AI to help you gain clarity, vision, and purpose to embrace, create and live your vision?

1. Yes. All done, planned, documented & given me fire in my belly.

2. On the case. Working towards it, gaining more clarity daily.

3. Oops. No, not yet completed (or started).

4. This is all too overwhelming. I Need help with this – fast.

Your Business Idea

Having a good and unique business idea that solves customer needs, pains, and frustrations is essential for sustaining growth in a competitive market. A good business idea can differentiate a company from its competitors and attract potential customers. A unique and disruptive business idea can create a buzz in the market and generate media attention, leading to increased brand awareness and credibility.

Furthermore, a good business idea can ensure a sustainable future for the company by solving real customer problems and meeting their needs. It can help establish a loyal customer base, generate positive reviews, and build a positive reputation. This, in turn, can lead to repeat business, referrals, and new customer acquisition, contributing to long-term success.

Having a unique, disruptive, and customer-focused business idea is critical for achieving sustained growth and success in today's competitive market. It sets a company apart from its competitors, generates buzz and media attention, and ensures the company's sustainability by solving real customer problems and meeting their needs.

Here are a few suggestions to help address common business and product name challenges and how you can ask, prompt, or instruct AI to assist you in achieving your goals and objectives on time, within budget and without quibble.

Each of the points below are split into 4 parts.

- **Challenge:** common issue or obstacle often faced by business owners
- **Fraserism:** a helpful hint, tip, quote, or suggestion to help you in overcoming a challenge.
- **Potential Prompt:** a question, task, and prompt to ask your preferred ai-powered VA.

- **Benefit:** The potential benefit of researching, documenting, executing, automating, and refining a task, process, procedure, or workflow that addresses the underlying challenge...

Challenge: **Does your product/service/business serve a presently un-served need?**
Fraserism: If the product/service/business does not serve an un-served need, it is important to conduct market research to identify any gaps in the market that could be filled. This could involve conducting surveys or focus groups to understand the needs and frustrations of potential customers.
Prompt: What steps can be taken to identify any un-served needs in the market?
Benefit: Conducting market research can help identify any gaps in the market and help businesses understand the needs and frustrations of potential customers. This can help businesses create products or services that are in demand and can ultimately lead to increased revenue and growth.

Challenge: **Does your solution serve an existing market where demand exceeds supply?**
Fraserism: If the solution does not serve an existing market where demand exceeds supply, it is important to consider whether the market can be expanded or whether a new market can be identified. This could involve developing new features or benefits that differentiate the product/service from competitors.
Prompt: What steps can be taken to identify existing markets where demand exceeds supply?
Benefit: Identifying existing markets where demand exceeds supply can help businesses create products or services that are in demand and can ultimately lead to increased revenue and growth.

Challenge: **Is your solution competitive because of an original & unique advantage?**
Fraserism: If the solution is not competitive because of an original & unique commercial advantage, it is important to consider what unique features or benefits the product/service can offer. This could involve developing a unique selling proposition (USP) that differentiates the

product/service from competitors.

Prompt: What steps can be taken to develop a unique selling proposition for a product or service?

Benefit: Developing a unique selling proposition can help businesses stand out from competitors and can ultimately lead to increased revenue and growth.

Challenge: Have you determined the resources you will need to start up the business?

Fraserism: If the resources needed to start up the business have not been determined, it is important to create a detailed list of all the resources needed, including equipment, supplies, and personnel. This can help businesses create a realistic budget and ensure that all necessary resources are available when needed.

Prompt: What steps can be taken to determine the resources needed to start up a business?

Benefit: Determining the resources needed to start up a business can help businesses create a realistic budget and ensure that all necessary resources are available when needed.

Challenge: Have you determined what your "survival" income is for the next 12 months?

Fraserism: If the "survival" income for the next 12 months has not been determined, it is important to create a detailed budget that takes into account all expected expenses and revenues. This can help businesses ensure that they have enough income to cover their expenses and keep the business running.

Prompt: What steps can be taken to determine the "survival" income for the next 12 months?

Benefit: Determining the "survival" income for the next 12 months can help tremendously, and I would recommend producing a monthly budget, networth statement and how much you owe and to whom.

Challenge: You are unsure how many leads you need to achieve your desired revenue.

Fraserism: To determine the number of leads you need, you should calculate your sales conversion rate and average order value. Once you know these numbers, you can estimate the number of leads you need to achieve your desired revenue. For example, if your conversion rate is 10% and your average order value is $100, you would need 1,000 leads to generate $10,000 in revenue.

Prompt: "How can I calculate the number of leads I need to achieve my desired revenue?"

Benefit: This prompt can help you set realistic revenue goals and create a more effective sales strategy.

Challenge: **You don't know how much website traffic you need to achieve your revenue goals.**

Fraserism: To estimate the website traffic you need, you should calculate your website's conversion rate and average order value. For instance, if your website conversion rate is 5% and your average order value is $50, you would need 2,000 website visitors to generate $5,000 in revenue.

Prompt: "How can I estimate the amount of website traffic I need to achieve my desired revenue?"

Benefit: This prompt can help you set realistic traffic goals and optimize your website for conversion.

Challenge: **You don't know how many referrals you need to achieve your desired revenue.**

Fraserism: To calculate the number of referrals you need, you should know your referral conversion rate, average order value, and referral rate. For example, if your referral conversion rate is 20%, your average order value is $75, and your referral rate is 10%, you would need 278 referrals to generate $5,000 in revenue.

Prompt: "How can I determine the number of referrals I need to achieve my desired revenue?"

Benefit: This prompt can help you create a referral program that can drive more business and revenue to your company.

Challenge: **You are unsure of the hardware, software, pinkware, and netware required for your business.**

Fraserism: To identify the tools and technology you need for your business, you should conduct research and seek guidance from experts in your industry. You can also consider your business goals and customer needs to determine the software and hardware requirements. For example, if you plan to sell products online, you will need e-commerce software and a website that can process payments securely.

Prompt: "How can I determine the necessary hardware, software, pinkware, and netware for my business?"

Benefit: This prompt can help you identify the right tools and technology to run your business more efficiently and effectively.

Challenge: **You don't know how to generate traffic and signups via your website.**

Fraserism: To generate traffic and signups, you can use various digital marketing strategies such as SEO, PPC advertising, social media, and email marketing. You can also optimize your website for conversion, create compelling content, and offer incentives to attract visitors and encourage signups.

Prompt: "What are the effective ways to generate traffic and signups via my website?"

Benefit: This prompt can help you attract more visitors to your website and generate more leads and conversions.

Challenge: **You can't communicate your business idea succinctly, fluently, and professionally.**

Fraserism: To communicate your business idea effectively, you should create an elevator pitch that describes your product or service, target audience, and unique value proposition in a concise and compelling way. You can also practice your presentation skills and use clear and professional language that resonates with your audience.

Prompt: "How can I effectively communicate my business idea?"

Benefit: This prompt can help you make a strong impression on potential customers, investors, and partners and increase the chances of success for your business

 Q. Does your business idea stack up? Does it make sense to potential stakeholders, shareholders, and investors when you share the concept? Do you use AI to help you gain clarity, vision, and purpose to embrace, create and live your vision?

1. Yes. All done, I am on point, on form and on fire.

2. On the case. Working towards it, documenting it.

3. Oops. No, not yet completed (or started).

4. This is all too overwhelming. I Need help with this – fast.

Nokia was a leading mobile phone manufacturer with a peak revenue of $51 billion in 2007. However, Nokia failed to keep up with the rapidly changing smartphone market and the emergence of touchscreens and app stores.
Competitors like Apple and Samsung gained a foothold in the market, and Nokia eventually sold its mobile phone business to Microsoft in 2014.

Get AI-powered help to save time, money & stress to do the jobs you hate, don't have time for, or simply don't want to do.

Reduce costs, improve efficiency & ROI to achieve your goals & objectives. It's your business. you're in control. You make the decisions.

You decide what you want to achieve next.

Sacrifices You Might Need to Make

Many people must make sacrifices in the early days of starting and running a business to stay within their means, cover expenses, and survive in that first year of starting a business. Sacrifices may include foregoing luxuries and cutting back on personal expenses. This may be difficult, but it is essential to keep costs low and maximize available resources. It may also require sacrificing personal time and working long hours, as well as taking on multiple roles within the business.

By making these sacrifices, entrepreneurs can keep their expenses under control and conserve their limited resources. This can increase the chances of long-term success by allowing the business to weather the inevitable challenges that come with starting a new venture. Additionally, by demonstrating a willingness to make sacrifices, entrepreneurs can inspire their team to do the same and show investors and other stakeholders that they are committed to the success of the business.

One potential benefit of making sacrifices in the early days is that it can help to build a strong foundation for future success and is a constant reminder not to be extravagant or waste your financial resources and available funds. By keeping costs low and conserving resources, entrepreneurs can position their business for growth and scalability.

They can also develop a culture of frugality and resourcefulness, which can help the business to continue to operate efficiently as it grows. Having said that, using AI to assist you identify the sacrifices you need to make or areas you can save money can often yield some surprising and life changing results.

Here are a few suggestions to help you recognize some sacrifices you need to make and how you can ask, prompt, or instruct AI to assist you in getting started with your business on time, within budget and without quibble.

Each of the points below are split into 4 parts.
- **Challenge:** common issue or obstacle often faced by business owners
- **Fraserism:** a helpful hint, tip, quote, or suggestion to help you in overcoming a challenge.
- **Potential Prompt:** a question, task, and prompt to ask your preferred ai-powered VA.
- **Benefit:** The potential benefit of researching, documenting, executing, automating, and refining a task, process, procedure, or workflow that addresses the underlying challenge.

Challenge: **Giving up a secure income can be daunting**
Fraserism: Start by creating a realistic financial plan that considers your expenses and projected income. This can help you identify areas where you may need to cut back and where you can afford to invest more in your business.
Potential prompt: How can I create a realistic financial plan to help me prepare for the transition to running my own business?
Benefit: By creating a realistic financial plan, you can identify potential financial challenges and develop strategies to address them, which can help you feel more confident and prepared for the transition to running your own business.

Challenge: **Giving up a predictable work schedule can affect your work life balance**
Fraserism: Consider setting clear boundaries between work and personal time, such as setting specific work hours or taking regular breaks throughout the day to recharge.
Potential prompt: What strategies can I use to balance my work and personal commitments when running my own business?
Benefit: By setting clear boundaries and balancing your work and personal commitments, you can reduce stress and increase productivity, which can help you achieve your business goals more effectively.

Challenge: **Giving up the opportunity to buy a new car can be disappointing**

Fraqserism: Consider exploring more affordable options, such as purchasing a used car or using public transportation instead.

Potential prompt: What are some affordable transportation options I can consider when starting my own business?

Benefit: By exploring more affordable transportation options, you can free up more of your budget to invest in your business, which can help you achieve your goals more quickly.

Challenge: **Giving up luxuries and home comforts can be difficult**

Fraserism: Identify the luxuries and home comforts that are most important to you and consider finding more affordable alternatives or ways to reduce your spending on these items.

Potential prompt: How can I reduce my spending on luxuries and home comforts without sacrificing too much comfort and security?

Benefit: By finding more affordable alternatives and reducing your spending on luxuries and home comforts, you can free up more of your budget to invest in your business, which can help you achieve your goals more quickly.

Challenge: **Giving up foreign holidays can be disappointing**

Fraserism: Consider exploring more affordable holiday options, such as taking a staycation or finding cheaper travel options.

Potential prompt: What are some affordable holiday options I can consider when starting my own business?

Benefit: By exploring more affordable holiday options, you can free up more of your budget to invest in your business, which can help you achieve your goals more quickly.

Challenge: **Sacrificing some of your personal comfort during the start-up phase**

Fraserism: Consider developing a self-care routine that includes stress-reducing activities, such as exercise, meditation, or spending time in nature.

Potential prompt: What are some effective stress-reducing activities I can incorporate into my daily routine when running my own business?

Benefit: By developing a self-care routine that includes stress-reducing activities, you can improve your overall well-being and be better equipped to handle the challenges of running your own business.

Challenge: **Waiting 30-45 days or longer to get paid for work done**
Fraserism: Offer incentives for early payment or negotiate shorter payment terms with clients. For example, offer a discount for payment within 14 days or negotiate payment terms of 15 days instead of 30.
Potential Prompt: "What steps can I take to encourage clients to pay earlier or even better, in advance.?"
Benefit: By offering incentives for early payment or negotiating shorter payment terms, businesses can improve their cash flow and reduce the risk of financial strain.

Challenge: **Financing the business out of your own pocket**
Fraserism: Investigate alternative financing options such as loans or crowdfunding. Start small and reinvest profits into the business to fuel growth. Send an offer to your LinkedIn network □
Potential Prompt: "What alternative financing options can I explore besides funding the business out of my own pocket?"
Benefit: By exploring alternative financing options, businesses can reduce the financial burden on the owner and increase their chances of success by having access to more resources.

Challenge: **Sharing profit to get financing or funding**
Fraserism: Consider equity financing or joint venture partnerships where profits are shared in exchange for funding. Ensure that any agreements are made in writing and clearly outline profit-sharing terms.
Potential Prompt: "What are some options for getting financing or funding without having to share a significant portion of the profits?"
Benefit: By exploring financing options that do not require sharing profits, businesses can retain more control over their operations and retain a larger portion of their profits.

Challenge: **Doing a lot of admin or financial record keeping**
Fraserism: Invest in financial software or hire an accountant to help with financial record keeping. Set aside dedicated time each week to stay on top of administrative tasks.
Potential Prompt: "What are some ways to streamline administrative and financial record-keeping tasks?"
Benefit: By investing in financial software or hiring an accountant, businesses can reduce the time and effort required for administrative tasks, allowing them to focus on other important aspects of the business.

Challenge: **Giving up sick pay when unable to work due to illness**
Fraserism: Consider purchasing private health insurance to provide coverage for lost income due to illness. Build up an emergency fund to cover unexpected financial gaps.
Prompt: "How can I prepare for the possibility of needing time off due to illness?"
Benefit: By having a plan in place for lost income due to illness, business owners can reduce the financial strain caused by unexpected time off.

Challenge: **Chasing people for money owed**
Fraserism: Set clear payment terms and follow up with clients who have outstanding invoices. Consider using a debt collection agency for more difficult cases.
Potential Prompt: "What are some strategies for collecting outstanding payments from clients?"
Benefit: By implementing clear payment terms and following up on outstanding invoices, businesses can improve cash flow and reduce the risk of financial strain caused by unpaid bills.

Challenge: **Using personal or partner's savings to get up and running**
Fraserism: Explore alternative financing options or start small and reinvest profits into the business to fuel growth. Consider creating a separate business bank account to help manage finances.
Potential Prompt: "What are some ways to reduce the reliance on personal savings to fund the business?"
Benefit: By exploring alternative financing options or reinvesting

profits, businesses can reduce the financial burden on the owner and increase their chances of success.

Challenge: **Giving up a quiet work area to work with kids running around**
Fraserism: Having worked from home for 20 years and had 5 kids, set boundaries, and established a dedicated workspace, set up a home office, to help reduce distractions. Consider hiring a babysitter or childcare provider during work hours on certain days and times.
Potential Prompt: "How can I create a productive work environment with children at home?"
Benefit: By creating a dedicated workspace and establishing

Q. What sacrifices do you (or will you) make when starting or running a business? Does it make sense to you and your family (and your bank manager) when you share your intentions? Do you use AI to help you gain clarity, vision, and purpose to embrace, create and live your vision?

1. Yes. All done, I am on point, on form and on fire.
2. On the case. Working towards it, documenting it.
3. Oops. No, not yet completed (or started).
4. This is all too overwhelming. I Need help with this – fast.

Sears was a major American department store chain
with a peak revenue of $53 billion in 2006
and over 300,000 employees.

However, Sears failed to adapt to the rise of e-commerce and
online shopping, leading to declining sales and profits.
Competitors like Amazon and Walmart were able to capture more
and more of the retail market share. In 2018, Sears filed
for bankruptcy and began closing hundreds of stores.

Get AI-powered help to save time, money & stress to do the
jobs you hate, don't have time for, or simply don't want to do.

Reduce costs, improve efficiency & ROI to achieve your
goals & objectives. It's your business. you're in control.
You make the decisions.

You decide what you want to achieve next.

Your Financial Position

Before starting a business, it's essential to have a solid understanding of your financial situation. It's like going on a road trip - you need to know how much gas you have in the tank and how far you can go before you need to refuel. In the same way, you need to know your income, expenses, and debt level to assess your financial capacity and determine how far your resources can take you.

Creating a budget is a crucial step in managing your finances. It's like creating a map for your road trip, helping you stay on track and reach your destination without running out of gas. Your budget should factor in your income and expenses, considering the cost of starting and running your business. This will help you identify areas where you can cut back on expenses and free up more capital for your business.

Debt can be a major obstacle when starting a business. It's like carrying a heavy load on your road trip - it slows you down and makes it harder to reach your destination. That's why it's important to understand your level of debt and develop a plan to reduce it. This will not only improve your financial position but also increase your chances of securing financing from lenders or investors.

Proper financial management is key to the success of any business. It's like maintaining your vehicle during your road trip - it helps ensure a smooth and safe journey. By managing your finances effectively, you can avoid financial pitfalls, stay within your budget, and set your business up for long-term success.

I cover this in more detail in my other book and share some excellent resources inside it:

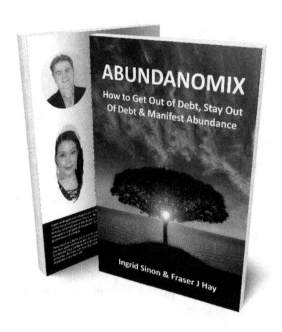

ABUNDANOMIX

How to Get Out of Debt, Stay Out Of Debt & Manifest Abundance

Ingrid Sinon & Fraser J Hay

AVAILABLE ON AMAZON

In short, understanding your financial position, managing your monthly budget, and knowing how much debt you are in before starting a business is mission critical. It will help you avoid financial difficulties, make informed decisions, and ensure you remain on point, on form and on fire.

Here are a few suggestions in response to common Entrepreneurial challenges and how to leverage AI to your advantage in helping you manage your financial situation when starting a business.

Each of the points below are split into 4 parts.

- **Challenge:** common issue or obstacle often faced by business owners
- **Fraserism:** a helpful hint, tip, quote, or suggestion to help you in overcoming a challenge.

- **Potential Prompt:** a question, task, and prompt to ask your preferred ai-powered VA.
- **Benefit:** The potential benefit of researching, documenting, executing, automating, and refining a task, process, procedure, or workflow that addresses the underlying challenge.

Challenge: **Not knowing your current financial situation**
Fraserism: I would recommend that you start by taking a thorough inventory of your current financial situation, including all your assets, liabilities, and expenses. This will help you get a clear picture of your financial standing and allow you to make informed decisions about your business.
Prompt: Can you tell me about your current financial situation, including your assets, liabilities, and expenses?
Benefit: By understanding your current financial situation, you can make informed decisions about your business and avoid taking on more risk than you can manage.

Challenge: **Not knowing all the costs associated with starting or running your business**
Fraserism: I would recommend that you take some time to identify all the costs associated with starting and running your business, including fixed costs like rent and salaries, and variable costs like inventory and marketing.
Prompt: Have you identified all the costs associated with starting and running your business? If not, what steps will you take to do so?
Benefit: By identifying all the costs associated with your business, you can create a more accurate budget and avoid running into unexpected expenses.

Challenge: **Not knowing budget for the first year of your business**
Fraserism: I would recommend that you create a detailed budget for the first year of your business, considering all your expected expenses and revenue.
Prompt: What is your budget for the first year of your business? Can you walk me through your expenses and revenue projections?
Benefit: Creating a detailed budget will help you stay on track financially and avoid overspending.

Challenge: **Not knowing what your projected revenues are for the first year**

Fraserism: I would recommend that you create a detailed revenue forecast for the first year of your business, considering all your expected income streams.

Potential Prompt: What are your projected revenue streams for the first year of your business? How did you arrive at these projections?
Benefit: Creating a revenue forecast will help you set realistic financial goals and plan for growth.

Challenge: **Not knowing the risks and challenges to your financial position**
Fraserism: I would recommend that you take some time to identify and assess any potential risks or challenges to your financial position, such as changes in the market or unexpected expenses.
Potential Prompt: Have you considered any potential risks or challenges to your financial position? How do you plan to address these risks?
Benefit: By identifying potential risks and challenges, you can create contingency plans and mitigate the impact of unexpected events.

Challenge: **Not knowing your financial plans for the next 12 months**
Fraserism: I would recommend that you set specific and measurable financial goals for your business, such as achieving a certain level of revenue or profit.
Potential Prompt: What are your financial goals for the first year of your business? How will you measure your progress towards these goals?
Benefit: Setting clear financial goals will help you stay focused and motivated and allow you to track your progress and adjust as needed.

Challenge: **Not having a projected cashflow for the next 12 months**
Fraserism: I would recommend that you create a detailed cash flow forecast for the first year of your business, considering all your

expected income and expenses.

Potential Prompt: Do you have a cash flow forecast for the first year of your business? Can you walk me through your expected cash flow?

Benefit: Creating a cash flow forecast will help you manage your finances more effectively and avoid cash flow problems.

Challenge: **Not knowing how much debt you have and to whom**

Fraserism: Carrying a significant amount of debt can be a hindrance to starting a business. Before starting a business, it's important to evaluate your current debt load and determine if it's feasible to take on additional debt to finance the business. One way to reduce debt is to create a debt repayment plan that focuses on paying off high-interest debt first.

Potential Prompt: What is the total amount of your outstanding debt and what types of debt do you have?

Benefit: By having a plan to reduce debt before starting a business, you can improve your chances of being approved for a business loan and reduce your financial stress.

Challenge: **Not having a plan to manage your personal finances while starting a business**

Fraserism: Starting a business can be a significant financial investment, and it's important to have a plan for managing personal finances during this time. One way to manage personal finances while starting a business is to create a budget that includes all personal expenses and identifies areas where expenses can be reduced.

Potential Prompt: What steps have you taken to create a budget that includes personal expenses and business expenses?

Benefit: By having a plan to manage personal finances while starting a business, you can reduce financial stress and focus on growing your business.

Challenge: **Not knowing your credit score**

Fraserism: Your credit score is an essential factor in obtaining financing for a business. Before applying for a business loan, it's important to know your credit score and work to improve it if necessary. One way to improve your credit score is to make sure all bills are paid on time.

Potential Prompt: What is your current credit score and what steps have you taken to improve it?

Benefit: By improving your credit score before starting a business, you can increase your chances of being approved for financing and potentially qualify for better loan terms.

Challenge: **Not knowing what the impact of starting a business can have on your credit score**

Fraserism: Starting a business can impact your personal credit score, and it's important to understand how this can happen. For example, if you use personal credit cards to finance the business, this can impact your credit utilization ratio and potentially lower your credit score.

Potential Prompt: Have you considered the potential impact of starting a business on your personal credit score and what steps have you taken to minimize this impact?

Benefit: By understanding the potential impact of starting a business on your personal credit, you can take steps to minimize this impact and protect your credit score.

Challenge: **Offering credit to others and the impact it will have on your cashflow**

Fraserism: In business, cash is king, and the quicker you can get it and keep it the better it will be for you. You want to get paid as quickly as possible, ideally up front.

Potential Prompt: Do you have any personal assets that could be used as capital for your business, and what risks do you see in using these assets?

Benefit: By evaluating personal assets as a potential source of capital for the business, you can reduce the need for outside financing and potentially retain

 Q. Do your maths stack up? Have you created a sales forecast, monthly budget, networth statement and creditor statement? Do you use AI to help you gain clarity, vision, and purpose to embrace, create and live your vision?

1. Yes. All done, I am on point, on form and on fire.

2. On the case. Working towards it, documenting it.

3. Oops. No, not yet completed (or started).

4. This is all too overwhelming. I Need help with this – fast.

BlackBerry was a dominant player in the smartphone industry in the early 2000s, with a peak revenue of $20 billion in 2011 and over 17,000 employees.

However, BlackBerry failed to keep up with the rise of touchscreens and app stores, and stuck with its physical keyboard and proprietary operating system. Competitors like Apple and Samsung quickly gained ground, and BlackBerry eventually stopped producing its own smartphones and shifted its focus to software and services.

Get AI-powered help to save time, money & stress to do the jobs you hate, don't have time for, or simply don't want to do.

Reduce costs, improve efficiency & ROI to achieve your goals & objectives. It's your business. you're in control. You make the decisions.

You decide what you want to achieve next.

A Disruptive Business Model?

In today's highly competitive business world, business owners to think outside the box to gain a competitive edge over their rivals. Disruptive business models can help businesses achieve this by revolutionizing entire industries and providing innovative solutions to meet customer needs. Here are some examples of how big companies have used disruptive business models to change traditional industries and stay ahead of the curve:

In the past, renting a movie meant physically visiting a video store, browsing through shelves of DVDs, and paying a rental fee. Netflix's subscription-based streaming service disrupted this traditional model by allowing customers to stream movies and TV shows directly to their devices. This not only provided greater convenience for customers, but it also disrupted the video rental industry by forcing brick-and-mortar stores like Blockbuster out of business.

Amazon's vast online marketplace disrupted the traditional retail industry by providing customers with access to a wide selection of products at competitive prices, all from the comfort of their own homes. This business model challenged the traditional brick-and-mortar retail stores, which had to adapt by offering online shopping options.

The traditional taxi industry was dominated by licensed cab drivers who had to be hailed on the street or through a phone call. Uber disrupted this model by offering a ride-sharing service that allowed customers to book rides directly from their smartphones. This provided greater convenience and affordability for customers, while challenging the traditional taxi industry.

The hotel industry was dominated by large hotel chains, making it difficult for homeowners to compete. Airbnb's platform disrupted this traditional model by offering homeowners a platform to rent out their properties as short-term rentals to travelers. This not only provided more affordable and unique accommodations for travelers, but it also challenged the traditional hotel industry.

By disrupting traditional business models, these companies were able to stand out from their competitors and create new opportunities for growth and success. As the business world continues to evolve, it is important for companies to embrace disruptive business models and stay ahead of the curve to remain competitive.

But what about you? Having a disruptive business model is essential for standing out from competitors and creating a unique value proposition for customers. By incorporating AI into their business model, businesses can streamline their operations, automate tasks, and make more informed decisions based on data analysis. This can lead to increased success, growth opportunities, and interest from investors and stakeholders.

Each of the points below are split into 4 parts.

- **Challenge:** common issue or obstacle often faced by business owners
- **Fraserism:** a helpful hint, tip, quote, or suggestion to help you in overcoming a challenge.
- **Potential Prompt:** a question, task, and prompt to ask your preferred ai-powered VA.
- **Benefit:** The potential benefit of researching, documenting, executing, automating, and refining a task, process, procedure, or workflow that addresses the underlying challenge.

Challenge: **Have you documented and automated key elements of your business model?**

Fraserism: Documenting and automating your business model can help you stay organized and efficient, enabling you to scale and grow your business. This can be achieved through process mapping and automation tools, such as Zapier or Integromat, to streamline workflows and reduce manual efforts.

Potential Prompt: Have you identified and documented the key processes and workflows in your business? How can you automate these processes to increase efficiency and scalability?

Benefit: Documenting and automating your business model can help you save time and resources, increase efficiency, and scale your business faster.

Challenge: **Have you documented & automated your customer journey and martech stack?**
Fraserism: Documenting your customer journey and martech stack can help you better understand your customers and optimize your marketing and sales efforts. This can be achieved through customer journey mapping and the use of martech tools at itstacksup.com to automate and optimize your marketing and sales processes.

Potential Prompt: Have you mapped out your customer journey and identified the key touchpoints? How can you optimize your martech stack to improve your customer experience and increase conversions?

Benefit: Documenting your customer journey and martech stack can help you increase customer engagement and conversions, improve customer experience, and boost sales.

Challenge: **Have you documented and automated your sales and marketing strategy?**

Fraserism: Documenting and automating your sales and marketing strategy can help you optimize your lead generation and conversion efforts. This can be achieved using marketing automation tools available on itstacksup.com to streamline your marketing campaigns and lead nurturing efforts.

Potential Prompt: Have you identified your target market and developed a marketing strategy to reach them? How can you automate your sales and marketing efforts to improve lead generation and conversion?

Benefit: Documenting and automating your sales and marketing strategy can help you save time and resources, increase lead generation and conversion, and grow your business faster.

Challenge: **Have you documented your mission and vision?**
Fraserism: It's important to clearly define and document your mission and vision so that everyone in the organization is aligned and working towards the same goal. This helps to create a sense of purpose and direction in the business and ensures that everyone is working towards the same end goal.
Potential Prompt: "Can you explain the importance of documenting a business's mission and vision?"

Benefit: Having a clear mission and vision helps to focus the organization's efforts and resources towards achieving a common goal, which can lead to increased motivation, productivity, and success.

Challenge: **Inefficiencies, duplication of effort, poor profitability and wasted resources.**
Fraserism: Automating your business model can help to streamline processes, reduce costs, and increase efficiency. By automating repetitive and time-consuming tasks, you can free up your time and resources to focus on more important aspects of your business, such as strategy and growth.
Potential Prompt: "Why is it important to automate your business model?"

Benefit: Automating your business model can lead to increased efficiency and productivity, as well as cost savings and a competitive advantage over businesses that rely on manual processes.

Challenge: **disjointed and inconsistent customer experience.**
Fraserism: Documenting and automating your customer journey can help to create a more streamlined and consistent customer experience. By mapping out each touchpoint in the customer journey, you can identify areas for improvement and optimize the customer experience. Automating certain aspects of the customer journey, such as email marketing and customer service, can also help to reduce response times and increase customer satisfaction.

Potential Prompt: "How can documenting and automating the customer journey benefit a business?"

Benefit: Documenting and automating the customer journey can lead to increased customer satisfaction and loyalty, as well as improved efficiency and cost savings for the business.

Challenge: **Your business values and a lack of consistency and alignment**
Fraserism: Defining and documenting your business values can help to create a shared sense of purpose and values within the organization. By communicating these values to employees and customers, you can create a consistent brand image and messaging that resonates with your target audience.
Potential Prompt: "What is the importance of defining and documenting a business's values?"

Benefit: Defining and documenting your business values can help to create a strong and consistent brand image, build customer loyalty, and attract like-minded employees who are aligned with your values.

Challenge: **Not creating a customer avatar and ideal client profile**
Fraserism: Creating a customer avatar and ideal client profile can help to create a clear understanding of your target audience and their needs. This can help to inform your marketing strategy and messaging and ensure that you are reaching the right people with the right message.
Potential Prompt: "What is the importance of creating a customer avatar and ideal client profile?"

Benefit: Creating a customer avatar and ideal client profile can lead to more effective marketing, improved customer targeting, and increased customer loyalty.

Challenge: **processes and workflows not streamlined and automated**
Fraserism: Identifying processes and workflows to be streamlined and automated can help to increase efficiency and reduce costs. By identifying areas for improvement and automating repetitive tasks,

you can free up your time and resources to focus on more important aspects of your business, such as strategy and growth.

Potential Prompt: "How can identifying processes and workflows to be streamlined and automated benefit a business?"

Benefit: Identifying processes and

Challenge: **Do you eliminate something for clients that your competitors can't or don't?**

Fraserism: One way to eliminate something for clients that competitors can't or don't is by offering a more personalized and tailored service to clients. This could mean creating a unique user experience or offering customized solutions to clients. For example, a company that offers a personalized skincare regimen based on a client's skin type and concerns would be eliminating the need for clients to search for products that work for them.

Potential Prompt: Can you provide an example of how you personalize your services for clients to set yourself apart from competitors?

Benefit: By providing a more personalized service, businesses can build stronger relationships with their clients, which can lead to increased loyalty and repeat business.

Challenge: **Do you reduce something for clients that your competitors can't or don't?**

Fraserism: One way to reduce something for clients that competitors can't or don't is by streamlining processes and reducing overhead costs. By doing so, businesses can pass the savings onto their clients, offering more affordable prices without sacrificing quality. For example, a company that uses automated systems to manage inventory and reduce waste could offer lower prices to clients than a competitor that relies on manual processes.

Potential Prompt: Can you provide an example of how you've streamlined your processes to reduce costs for clients?

Benefit: By offering more affordable prices, businesses can attract price-sensitive clients and gain a competitive advantage over their competitors.

Challenge: **Do you create something for clients that your competitors can't or don't?**

Fraserism: One way to create something for clients that competitors can't or don't is by offering new and innovative products or services that solve a problem or meet a need that is not currently being addressed in the market. For example, a company that creates eco-friendly alternatives to common household products could attract environmentally conscious clients who are not currently being served by their competitors.

Potential Prompt: Can you provide an example of how you've developed a product or service that is unique in the market?

Benefit: By offering unique products or services, businesses can attract new clients and differentiate themselves from their competitors.

Challenge: **Do you have innovative and automated ways to increase customer lifetime value?**

Fraserism: One way to increase customer lifetime value is by implementing innovative and automated systems that keep clients engaged and satisfied with the company's products or services. For example, a company that uses a customer loyalty program or offers personalized product recommendations could increase customer lifetime value by encouraging repeat purchases.

Potential Prompt: Can you provide an example of how you use automation to increase customer lifetime value?

Benefit: By increasing customer lifetime value, businesses can generate more revenue and improve their bottom line.

Challenge: **Do you have strategic channel partners that your competitors don't?**

Fraserism: One way to set yourself apart from competitors is by forming strategic partnerships or channel partnerships that provide unique opportunities to generate revenue or expand your customer base. For example, a company that partners with a complementary business to offer a bundle package could attract new clients who are interested in both products and services.

Potential Prompt: Can you provide an example of a strategic partnership or channel partnership that has benefited your business?

Benefit: By forming strong partnerships, businesses can gain access to new markets

73

Q. Have you automated key elements of your business model? Do you use AI to streamline your processes, workflows and differentiate you and your business in the marketplace? Do you use AI to help you gain clarity, vision, and purpose to embrace, create and live your vision?

 1. Yes. All done, planned, documented & included in our business plan.
 2. On the case. Working towards it, documenting it.
 3. Oops. No, not yet completed (or started).
 4. This is all too overwhelming. I Need help with this – fast.

START-UP

Your Business Plan

Writing a business plan is like building a house - you need a solid foundation to support the structure and ensure it can withstand external pressures. Just as a blueprint guides the construction of a house, a business plan serves as a roadmap for your business and outlines its goals, strategies, and financial projections. But let's face it - creating a comprehensive business plan can be a daunting task, especially for entrepreneurs who may have limited resources and time.

Thankfully, AI can help streamline the process and alleviate some of the challenges of business planning. For instance, AI-powered tools can help you research the market and identify potential customers, competitors, and trends. They can also provide insights into financial projections and help you determine the viability of your business model.

Moreover, AI can assist you in documenting your business idea by generating a preliminary draft of your business plan. By using natural language processing and machine learning algorithms, AI can analyze your inputs and generate a coherent and well-structured business plan that aligns with your objectives and goals. You can then refine and customize the plan to suit your specific needs and preferences.

Ensuring you write a comprehensive business plan is essential for the success of your startup. Using AI can help you overcome some of the common challenges involved in business planning. By leveraging AI-powered tools, you can research, plan, and document your business idea more efficiently, saving you time and resources that you can invest in growing your business.

Each of the points below are split into 4 parts.

- **Challenge:** common issue or obstacle often faced by business owners
- **Fraserism:** a helpful hint, tip, quote, or suggestion to help

you in overcoming a challenge.

- **Potential Prompt:** a question, task, and prompt to ask your preferred ai-powered VA.
- **Benefit:** The potential benefit of researching, documenting, executing, automating, and refining a task, process, procedure, or workflow that addresses the underlying challenge.

Challenge: **Lack of clarity on the goals of the business plan.**
Fraserism: The purpose of a business plan is to provide a roadmap for the future of the business, outlining its objectives, strategies, and tactics for achieving success.
Potential Prompt: Can you describe the key objectives of your business plan?
Benefit: By having a clear understanding of the purpose of the business plan, you can ensure that it is focused, concise, and effective in achieving its intended goals. Who is your target audience for the business plan?

Challenge: **Not knowing the intended audience can result in an ineffective business plan.**
Fraserism: The target audience for a business plan could be potential investors, lenders, partners, or internal stakeholders. It's essential to tailor the plan to the specific needs and interests of the target audience.
Potential Prompt: Who will be reviewing your business plan, and what are their priorities?
Benefit: By understanding the target audience, you can better tailor the plan to their needs, increasing the likelihood of a successful outcome.
What problem does your business solve for its customers?

Challenge: **Not clearly defining the problem the business solves**
Fraserism: A business plan should clearly articulate the pain points of the target customer and how the business solves those problems in a unique and compelling way.
Potential Prompt: What are the key challenges faced by your target customer, and how does your business address these challenges?
Benefit: By clearly defining the problem your business solves, you

can better articulate its unique value proposition, making it more attractive to potential investors or partners.

Challenge: **Not having a clear unique value proposition**
Fraserism: The unique value proposition is a statement that describes the unique benefits of a business that sets it apart from competitors. It should be clear, concise, and compelling.
Potential Prompt: What sets your business apart from competitors, and how does it solve the problem differently?
Benefit: By clearly defining the unique value proposition, you can differentiate the business from competitors, making it more attractive to potential customers or investors.
What is your business model?

Challenge: **Not having a clear business model**
Fraserism: The business model describes how the business will create, deliver, and capture value. It should outline the key revenue streams, cost structures, and other key elements of the business.
Potential Prompt: How will your business generate revenue, and what are the key costs associated with running the business?
Benefit: By clearly defining the business model, you can better understand the financial viability of the business and identify potential areas for growth or improvement.
What are your revenue streams?

Challenge: **Not having clearly defined revenue streams**
Fraserism: Revenue streams describe the sources of income for the business, including sales of products or services, subscription fees, licensing fees, or other sources.
Potential Prompt: What are the key revenue streams for your business, and how do they contribute to the overall financial success of the business?
Benefit: By clearly defining the revenue streams, you can identify potential areas for growth and expansion, making the business more attractive to potential investors or partners.

Challenge: **Not knowing all your start-up costs and monthly operating costs**
Fraserism: It is important to have produced a monthly budget, net

worth statement, sales forecast, and an expenditure breakdown. Without a clear understanding of the numbers, it will be difficult to improve your situation and build a sustainable business.

Prompt: "Share an example profit and loss account, monthly budget, sales forecast and cashflow"

Benefit: You can tweak this example or use the one in my copy of "abundanomix" to help you. I also recommend investing in a good accounts package such as QuickBooks, Sage or xero.

Challenge: **Not knowing what lenders and investors like to see in a business plan.**

Fraserism: Lenders and investors want to see a clear and concise business plan that outlines the goals of the business, the market opportunity, the revenue streams, and the funding requirements. They also want to see that the business owner has a clear understanding of the market and the competition.

Prompt: "What do lenders and investors look for in a business plan?"

Benefit: Understanding what lenders and investors look for in a business plan will increase your chances of securing funding and making your business successful.

Challenge: **You may not know what should be included in their executive summary.**

Fraserism: The executive summary should provide a brief overview of the business plan and highlight the key points, such as the goals of the business, the market opportunity, the unique selling proposition, and the funding requirements. It should be clear, and compelling.

Prompt: "What should be included in the executive summary of a business plan?"

Benefit: A well-written executive summary will grab the attention of lenders and investors and encourage them to read the rest of your business plan.

Challenge: **You may not have documented the size of their market and whether it's growing**

Fraserism: It is important to document the size of the market and its growth potential to demonstrate the market opportunity for your business. This information will help you develop a targeted marketing plan and make informed decisions about your business strategy.

Prompt: "Why is it important to document the size of your market and whether it's growing or declining?"

Benefit: Documenting the size and growth potential of your market will help you make informed decisions about your business strategy and target the right audience with your marketing efforts.

Challenge: **You may not have documented the needs of the market and how you satisfy them**

Fraserism: Documenting the needs of the market and how you satisfy those needs will help you develop a targeted marketing plan and differentiate your business from the competition. It will also help you identify areas for improvement in your business offering.

Prompt: "Why is it important to document the needs of the market and how you satisfy those needs?"

Benefit: Documenting the needs of the market and how you satisfy those needs will help you develop a strong business offering and increase your chances of success.

Challenge: **You may not have documented your marketing & promotional activities calendar**

Fraserism: No, I haven't documented my marketing and promotional activities calendar yet. It's important to document all marketing and promotional activities in a calendar to stay organized and on track with marketing goals. This calendar should include dates, events, campaigns, and promotions. It's also important to assign responsibilities for each activity and ensure that all team members are aware of the marketing plan.

Potential Prompt: How do I ensure that I am organized and on track with my marketing goals?

Benefit: By documenting all marketing and promotional activities in a calendar, it ensures that you stay organized and on track with marketing goals. This can lead to a more successful marketing campaign and help increase sales and revenue for the business.

Q. Have you addressed key elements of your business plan? Do you use AI to streamline your processes, workflows and differentiate you and your business in the marketplace? Do you use AI to help you gain clarity, vision, and purpose to embrace, create and live your vision?

1. Yes. All done, planned, documented & included in our business plan.
2. On the case. Working towards it, documenting it.
3. Oops. No, not yet completed (or started).
4. This is all too overwhelming. I Need help with this – fast.

Xerox was a pioneer in the photocopier and printer industry, with a peak revenue of $19 billion in 1999 and over 140,000 employees.

However, Xerox failed to capitalize on its early innovations and was slow to embrace digital technology and the shift towards paperless offices. Competitors like HP and Canon were able to outpace Xerox in innovation and sales, and Xerox has since undergone several rounds of restructuring and divestitures.

Get AI-powered help to save time, money & stress to do the jobs you hate, don't have time for, or simply don't want to do.

Reduce costs, improve efficiency & ROI to achieve your goals & objectives. It's your business. you're in control. You make the decisions.

You decide what you want to achieve next.

GDPR

Safeguarding sensitive customer data is critical for organisations and complying with the General Data Protection Regulation (GDPR) is essential. The GDPR provides guidelines for collecting, processing, and storing personal data, and it is the responsibility of organizations to ensure that they protect it from unauthorized access, use, and disclosure. Failure to comply with GDPR regulations can result in severe penalties, including hefty fines and loss of customer trust.

To understand the importance of protecting customer data, let's consider an example. Imagine that you run a small e-commerce business, and you store your customers' personal and financial data on your website. If this data falls into the wrong hands due to a data breach or cyber-attack, it could have a severe impact on your business. Your customers' trust could be lost, and they may no longer feel safe sharing their personal and financial information with your company. This loss of trust could result in a significant drop in revenue and even the ultimate demise of your business.

Effective data protection measures are essential for preventing such scenarios. For example, you can think of data protection measures such as the locks on the doors and windows of a house. Just as locks prevent unauthorized entry into a home, access controls, encryption, and system audits prevent unauthorized access to customer data. It is also important to have clear data protection policies in place and to provide training for employees to ensure they understand their responsibilities. You could consider these policies as instructions or guidelines for using those locks effectively.

However, complying with GDPR regulations can be challenging, especially for small businesses that may not have the necessary resources or expertise. This is where AI can come in handy. By using AI to document and manage GDPR policies, processes, and procedures, organizations can save time and reduce the risk of errors or inconsistencies. AI can help address common GDPR challenges by providing prompts, instructions, and suggestions for achieving data protection goals and objectives.

For instance, AI can assist you in identifying the personal data they collect, where it's stored, and who has access to it. AI can also help in identifying the data that needs to be encrypted and ensuring that all employees are trained to handle such data properly. With AI, business can effectively manage their GDPR compliance and protect their customers' data while maintaining their reputation and building trust.

Each of the points below are split into 4 parts.

- **Challenge:** common issue or obstacle often faced by business owners
- **Fraserism:** a helpful hint, tip, quote, or suggestion to help you in overcoming a challenge.
- **Potential Prompt:** a question, task, and prompt to ask your preferred ai-powered VA.
- **Benefit:** The potential benefit of researching, documenting, executing, automating, and refining a task, process, procedure, or workflow that addresses the underlying challenge.

Challenge: **Not being aware of how the GDPR will affect your business.**
Fraserism: Research and understand the impact of the GDPR on your business. Visit www.ico.gov.uk and seek professional guidance to determine how your business can become GDPR compliant.
Potential Prompt: What steps should I take to understand the impact of the GDPR on my business?
Benefit: By becoming informed about the GDPR's impact on your business, you can avoid penalties and maintain customer trust.

Challenge: **Not familiar with the requirements of the GDPR.**
Fraserism: Research and understand the requirements of the GDPR. Create a plan to implement these requirements in your business operations.
Potential Prompt: What are the requirements of the GDPR, and how can I ensure that my business complies with them?
Benefit: By understanding the GDPR's requirements and

implementing them, you can ensure that your business complies with GDPR regulations and avoids penalties.

Challenge: **The Information Commissioner's Office.**
Fraserism: You should research the requirements and register with the Information Commissioner's Office if necessary. You could visit www.ico.org.uk
Potential Prompt: What are the requirements for registering with the Information Commissioner's Office and how can I ensure that my business is compliant?
Benefit: Registering with the Information Commissioner's Office can help you protect the personal information of your customers and comply with data protection laws.

Challenge: **Not having a plan to become compliant with GDPR.**
Fraserism: Develop a plan to become GDPR compliant. Identify the necessary steps, allocate resources, and establish timelines for achieving compliance.
Potential Prompt: How can I develop a plan to become GDPR compliant?
Benefit: By developing a plan to become GDPR compliant, you can ensure that your business is prepared to meet GDPR regulations and avoid penalties.

Challenge: **Not documented what personal data you hold**
Fraserism: Conduct a data audit to identify what personal data your business holds. Document the types of data, sources, and purposes for holding this data.
Potential Prompt: How can I document the personal data my business holds?
Benefit: By documenting what personal data your business holds, you can ensure that you have a clear understanding of the data you process and avoid unauthorized access or breaches.

Challenge: **Not documented where personal data you hold, came from**
Fraserism: Document the sources of personal data your business holds. This includes the data subject and any third-party sources.
Potential Prompt: How can I document the sources of personal data

my business holds?

Benefit: By documenting the sources of personal data your business holds, you can ensure transparency and accountability in your data processing operations.

Challenge: **Not documented whom you share personal data with**

Fraserism: Document the third parties with whom you share personal data, including the type of data and the purpose for sharing.

Potential Prompt: How can I document with whom my business shares personal data?

Benefit: By documenting with whom you share personal data, you can ensure that data protection measures are in place and that data is not shared beyond the scope of its intended purpose.

Challenge: **Not written or reviewed your privacy notices**

Fraserism: Review your current privacy notices to ensure that they comply with GDPR regulations. Identify areas for improvement and create a plan to update them.

Potential Prompt: How can I ensure that my business's privacy notices comply with GDPR regulations?

Benefit: By reviewing and updating your privacy notices, you can ensure transparency and accountability in your data processing operations and comply with GDPR regulations.

Challenge: **Not got a written plan for reviewing your privacy notices**

Fraserism: Develop a plan for updating your privacy notices to comply with GDPR regulations. This includes identifying areas for improvement, drafting new language, and communicating changes to customers.

Potential Prompt: How can I develop a plan for updating my privacy notices to comply with GDPR regulations?

Benefit: By developing a plan for updating your privacy notices, you can ensure that your customers are informed about how their data is processed and comply with GDPR regulations.

Challenge: **Not reviewed how you seek, record, and manage consent in your marketing funnel**

Fraserism: You should review your consent management process and update it to meet GDPR requirements. This could involve implementing an opt-in process for marketing communications and ensuring that you have a record of individuals' consent. Consider providing clear and easily accessible information about how you will use personal data and allowing individuals to withdraw their consent at any time.

Potential Prompt: How can I improve my consent management process to comply with GDPR?

Benefit: By implementing GDPR-compliant consent management processes, you can ensure that individuals' personal data is managed lawfully and transparently, which can help build trust and credibility with your customers and avoid potential fines or reputational damage.

Challenge: Not translated GDPR compliance into a practical plan to generate NEW leads

Fraserism: You should review your marketing strategies and develop a GDPR-compliant plan to generate new leads. This could involve identifying your target audience and finding creative ways to obtain their consent for marketing communications. Consider offering incentives or providing valuable content in exchange for consent.

Potential Prompt: How can I generate new leads while ensuring GDPR compliance?

Benefit: By developing a GDPR-compliant plan to generate new leads, you can build a strong pipeline of potential customers while demonstrating your commitment to data protection and compliance.

Challenge: Not written a marketing plan that will translate GDPR readiness into leads?

Fraserism: You should develop a GDPR-compliant marketing plan that aligns with your business goals and targets specific customer segments. This could involve conducting market research and developing a value proposition that resonates with your target audience. Consider using a mix of marketing channels and tactics, such as content marketing, social media advertising, and email marketing, to reach potential customers.

Potential Prompt: How can I develop a GDPR-compliant marketing plan that drives leads and sales?

Benefit: By developing a comprehensive marketing plan that aligns with GDPR requirements, you can build a strong pipeline of potential customers and drive revenue growth while mitigating legal and reputational risks.

Q. Have you documented your GDPR policies, processes, and SOPs? Do you use AI to document and manage your privacy centre, GDPR compliance throughout your business? Do you use AI to help you gain clarity, vision, and purpose to embrace, create and live your vision?

1. Yes. All done, planned, documented & included in our privacy centre.
2. On the case. Working towards it, documenting it.
3. Oops. No, not yet completed (or started).
4. This is all too overwhelming. I Need help with this – fast.

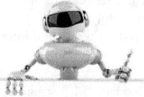

Toys "R" Us was a major toy retailer with a peak revenue of $13.6 billion in 1990 and over 60,000 employees.

However, Toys "R" Us failed to adapt to the rise of online shopping and the competition from e-commerce giants like Amazon. Despite efforts to revamp their online presence and improve customer experience, the company was unable to keep up and filed for bankruptcy in 2017, leading to the closure of all its stores.

Get AI-powered help to save time, money & stress to do the jobs you hate, don't have time for, or simply don't want to do.

Reduce costs, improve efficiency & ROI to achieve your goals & objectives. It's your business. you're in control. You make the decisions.

You decide what you want to achieve next.

Innovation

Innovation is like a key that unlocks the door to success and growth for businesses in today's dynamic and ever-changing market. It's like a secret recipe that adds flavor and uniqueness to your products or services. But just like any recipe, innovation can be complicated and risky. That's why it's essential to strike a balance between the need to innovate and the need to manage risk and profitability.

One way to achieve this balance is by leveraging the power of AI. AI can help businesses reduce waste, cut costs, streamline processes, and increase ROI, making it a valuable tool for achieving your innovation goals and objectives.

For example, let's say you want to innovate your production process to reduce waste and increase efficiency. You could ask an AI-powered system to analyze your data and identify areas of improvement, such as bottlenecks or inefficiencies in your supply chain. You could also prompt the AI to suggest alternative materials or processes that could reduce waste and improve product quality.

Or let's say you want to create a new product that will resonate with your target audience. You could instruct an AI-powered system to analyze market trends and consumer behavior to identify gaps in the market or areas where you could differentiate yourself from your competitors. The AI could also suggest product features or design elements that would appeal to your target audience.

By embracing AI and integrating it into your innovation strategy, you can foster a culture of innovation, stay ahead of the curve, and drive growth and success for your business.
Each of the points below are split into 4 parts.

- **Challenge:** common issue or obstacle often faced by business owners
- **Fraserism:** a helpful hint, tip, quote, or suggestion to help you in overcoming a challenge.

- **Potential Prompt:** a question, task, and prompt to ask your preferred ai-powered VA.
- **Benefit:** The potential benefit of researching, documenting, executing, automating, and refining a task, process, procedure, or workflow that addresses the underlying challenge.

Challenge: **Lack of innovation policy.**
Fraserism: Create an innovation policy that outlines the goals and objectives for innovation within the company, including the resources and support that will be provided.
Potential Prompt: What are the key objectives of your innovation policy, and how will they be measured and tracked?
Benefit: An innovation policy helps to ensure that the company is focused on creating new and innovative products, services, and processes, and that there is a clear plan in place to achieve these goals.

Challenge: **No innovation strategy document or "Master Plan".**
Fraserism: Develop an innovation strategy document that outlines the company's vision, goals, and objectives for innovation, as well as the specific tactics that will be used to achieve these goals.
Potential Prompt: What are the key elements of your innovation strategy, and how will they be implemented across the organisation?

Benefit: An innovation strategy document provides a clear roadmap for the company's innovation efforts, ensuring that everyone is aligned and working towards a common goal.

Challenge: **Lack of staff with innovative skills, talent, knowledge & experience.**
Fraserism: Develop a recruitment strategy that targets individuals with the necessary innovative skills, talent, knowledge, and experience, and invest in training and development programs to help current employees develop these skills.
Potential Prompt: How are you attracting and retaining innovative talent, and what training and development opportunities are available to help current employees develop these skills?

Benefit: Having a team with the right innovative skills and experience is essential for driving innovation within the company and staying competitive in the market.

Challenge: **No processes, procedures & methods in place to capture/create ideas.**
Fraserism: Develop a structured approach to idea generation and capture, such as brainstorming sessions, suggestion boxes, or regular ideation meetings.
Potential Prompt: What are the key methods you use to generate and capture new ideas, and how do you evaluate and prioritize these ideas?

Benefit: A structured approach to idea generation and capture ensures that the company is constantly generating new and innovative ideas that can be developed into new products, services, or processes.

Challenge: **No investment in training in areas like innovation, problem solving, marketing.**
Fraserism: Develop training programs that focus on key skills related to innovation, such as problem-solving, critical thinking, and creativity, as well as marketing and other business skills.
Potential Prompt: What training and development programs are available to help employees develop key skills related to innovation, problem-solving, and marketing?

Benefit: Investing in training and development programs helps to ensure that employees have the necessary skills and knowledge to drive innovation and stay competitive in the market.

Challenge: **No recruitment of staff from other countries.**
Fraserism: Develop a recruitment strategy that targets international talent and creates a diverse workforce with a range of perspectives and experiences.
Potential Prompt: What efforts are you making to attract international talent, and how are you creating a diverse and inclusive workforce?

Benefit: Hiring staff from other countries brings new perspectives and experiences to the company, which can help to drive innovation and improve the company's overall performance.

Challenge: **No research and development (R&D) within the organisation.**

Fraserism: Invest in R&D programs to explore new technologies, develop new products and services, and improve existing ones.

Potential Prompt: What R&D programs are in place, and how are they helping to drive innovation and improve the company's offerings?

Benefit: Investing in R&D programs helps to ensure that the company is constantly exploring new technologies and ideas, which can lead to new products, services, and processes that can drive growth and profitability.

Challenge: **Not implementing any new innovative practices can cause your business to become stagnant and less competitive.**

Fraserism: Set aside time to brainstorm new innovative ideas or attend workshops or seminars to learn about the latest trends and technologies. For example: "Can you suggest some workshops or seminars that would help me learn about the latest innovative practices in my industry?"

Benefit: By attending these events, you can gain new perspectives and knowledge to help spark innovative ideas and keep your business competitive.

Challenge: **Not researching customer needs or preferences can lead to missed opportunities for innovation that could meet their needs.**

Fraserism: Conduct customer surveys, focus groups, or other research methods to gain insights into customer needs and preferences. For example: "What are some effective research methods I can use to better understand my customers' needs and preferences?"

Benefit: By gaining a deeper understanding of your customers, you can identify new areas for innovation and create products or services that better meet their needs.

Challenge: **Not having a strategy to foster a culture of innovation can lead to a lack of focus and direction in your innovation efforts.**

Fraserism: Develop a clear innovation strategy and communicate it to your employees to create a culture of innovation. For example: "How can I develop an innovation strategy that will create a culture of innovation within my organization?"

Benefit: By creating a culture of innovation, your employees will be more likely to generate new ideas and collaborate to create innovative solutions.

Challenge: **Not allocating resources specifically for the purpose of innovation can hinder your ability to invest in new innovative ideas.**

Fraserism: Set aside a dedicated innovation budget or team to invest in new innovative ideas. For example: "How can I create a dedicated innovation budget or team to invest in new innovative ideas?"

Benefit: By allocating resources specifically for innovation, you can invest in new innovative ideas that have the potential to create significant returns on investment.

Challenge: **Not exploring potential collaborations with other companies or organizations can limit your exposure to new innovative ideas.**

Fraserism: Look for opportunities to collaborate with other companies or organizations to bring in new innovative ideas. For example: "Can you suggest some potential partners that I can collaborate with to bring new innovative ideas to my business?"

Benefit: By collaborating with other companies or organizations, you can gain access to new innovative ideas and expertise that you may not have within your own organization.

Challenge: **Not outsourcing certain tasks or projects to external partners can limit your exposure to fresh perspectives and expertise.**

Fraserism: Consider outsourcing certain tasks or projects to external partners to bring in fresh perspectives and expertise. For example: "What are some tasks or projects that I can outsource to external partners to bring in fresh perspectives and expertise?"

Benefit: By outsourcing certain tasks or projects, you can gain access to fresh perspectives and expertise that can help you generate new innovative ideas and solutions.

Challenge: **Not looking into adopting new technologies or tools can limit your ability to streamline processes and increase efficiency in your business.**

Fraserism: Explore new technologies or tools to streamline processes and increase efficiency in your business.

For example: "Can you suggest some new technologies or tools that I can adopt to streamline processes and increase efficiency in my business?"

Benefit: By adopting new technologies or tools, you can increase efficiency and productivity, which can free up time and resources to invest in new innovative ideas.

Q. Do you have an innovation strategy in your business? you use AI to document, manage and create new innovative technologies and strategies?? Do you use AI to help you gain clarity, vision, and purpose to embrace, create and live your vision?

1. Yes. All done, planned, documented & included in our business plan.

2. On the case. Working towards it, documenting it.

3. Oops. No, not yet completed (or started).

4. This is all too overwhelming. I Need help with this – fast.

Market Research

Market research is of utmost importance when starting and growing a business. The complexity of the business world demands that entrepreneurs gather all necessary information to make informed decisions. Market research provides this information, allowing entrepreneurs to identify and analyze consumer behavior, competitor activity, and market trends. With the help of market research, businesses can identify the demand for their products or services, understand their target audience, and create effective marketing strategies.

Moreover, market research is not only valuable when starting a business but also when growing it. As businesses expand, they encounter new challenges and opportunities, and it becomes even more important to stay abreast of market changes. Continual market research enables businesses to adjust their strategies, update their products or services, and respond to emerging trends. This helps businesses stay competitive, maximize their potential, and stay ahead of the curve.

In conclusion, market research is vital to the success of any business. It provides valuable insights and information that allow entrepreneurs to make informed decisions, identify and analyze consumer behavior and competitor activity, and create effective marketing strategies. Continual market research is necessary to adapt to changing market conditions, expand the business, and remain competitive in today's dynamic business world.

Having said that, you could use AI to help you to research your industry, sector or niche.to identify new sales and marketing opportunities. Here are a few suggestions to help address common market research challenges and how you can ask, prompt, or instruct AI to assist you in achieving your market research goals and objectives on time, within budget and without quibble.

Each of the points below are split into 4 parts.

- **Challenge:** common issue or obstacle often faced by business owners
- **Fraserism:** a helpful hint, tip, quote, or suggestion to help you in overcoming a challenge.
- **Potential Prompt:** a question, task, and prompt to ask your preferred ai-powered VA.
- **Benefit:** The potential benefit of researching, documenting, executing, automating, and refining a task, process, procedure, or workflow that addresses the underlying challenge.

Challenge: **missing potential opportunities**

Fraserism: Conduct market research and analyze consumer behavior to stay up to date on changes in the target market. Utilize surveys, customer feedback, and social media analytics to gain insight into shifting preferences and behaviors.

Potential Prompt: "What strategies do you recommend for staying informed about changes in the target market?"

Benefit: By staying aware of changes in the target market, businesses can adjust their marketing strategies, products or services, and communication to better meet the needs and wants of their audience.

Challenge: **Not knowing what products or services are in high demand within the industry**

Fraserism: Conduct market research to identify the top-selling products or services in the industry. Utilize industry reports, online marketplaces, and consumer feedback to gain insight into consumer preferences.

Potential Prompt: "What sources do you recommend for identifying the top-selling products or services in the industry?"

Benefit: Knowing the top-selling products or services can help businesses tailor their offerings and marketing strategies to better meet the needs and wants of their target audience.

Challenge: **Not having a clear understanding of the margin %**

Fraserism: Calculate the cost of goods sold (COGS) and subtract it from the sale price to determine the margin %. Ensure that the margin % is high enough to cover operating expenses and generate a profit.

Potential Prompt: "What factors should be considered when calculating the margin % for a product or service?"

Benefit: Understanding the margin % for each product or service can help businesses make informed pricing decisions, which can impact profitability and overall business success.

Challenge: **Not knowing what questions potential clients want answering**
Fraserism: Conduct keyword research and use tools like Google Trends or AnswerThePublic to identify common questions and search terms related to your industry or products.
Potential Prompt: "What are the most common questions or search terms potential clients use when looking for a solution like ours?"
Benefit: By knowing the questions potential clients are asking, you can tailor your marketing and messaging to address their specific needs and concerns.

Challenge: **Not knowing the demand for services can result in a lack of sales**
Fraserism: Conduct market research to determine the size of your target market, their buying habits, and the demand for your products and services.
Potential Prompt: "How large is our target market and what is the demand for our products and services?"
Benefit: By understanding the demand for your offerings, you can better allocate resources, adjust pricing, and target your marketing efforts to maximize sales.

Challenge: **Not knowing what keywords prospects are typing in to find your competitors**

Fraserism: Use tools like SEMrush or Ahrefs to identify the keywords and search terms your competitors are ranking for and incorporate them into your own SEO strategy.

Potential Prompt: "What keywords are our competitors using to rank highly in search engines?"

Benefit: By targeting the same keywords as your competitors, you can improve your search engine rankings, increase website traffic, and generate more leads.

Challenge: **Not knowing who your competitors are targeting and why**

Fraserism: Conduct competitor analysis to identify your main competitors, their target market, and their unique selling points.

Potential Prompt: "Who are our main competitors and who are they targeting with their marketing?"

Benefit: By understanding your competitors' target market and unique selling points, you can differentiate your offerings and tailor your marketing efforts to reach your own target audience more effectively.

Challenge: **Not knowing which channels your competitors are using to promote their services**

Fraserism: Analyze your competitors' marketing channels, such as social media, email marketing, or advertising, to identify which ones are most effective for reaching their target audience.

Potential Prompt: "What marketing channels are our competitors using to reach their target audience?"

Benefit: By identifying the most effective marketing channels, you can allocate your resources more efficiently and create a more effective marketing strategy.

Challenge: **Not knowing which engagement tactics your competitors are using**

Fraserism: Analyze your competitors' engagement tactics, such as customer reviews, social media interactions, or loyalty programs, to identify which ones are most effective for engaging with their audience.

Potential Prompt: "What engagement tactics are our competitors using to build relationships with their audience?"
Benefit: By identifying the most effective engagement tactics, you can create a more effective customer engagement strategy and build stronger relationships with your own audience.

Challenge: **Not knowing why prospective customers do business with your competitors**
Fraserism: Conduct customer research and analyze your competitors' unique selling points to identify why customers choose them over you.
Potential Prompt: "Why do prospective customers choose our competitors instead of us?"
Benefit: By understanding why customers choose your competitors, you can differentiate your offerings, improve your sales strategy, and better target your marketing efforts.

 Q. Do you have a market research strategy FOR your business? Do you use AI to help you find or create new sales opportunities? Do you use AI to help you gain clarity, vision, and purpose to embrace, create and live your vision?

1. Yes. All done, planned, documented & included in our business plan.
2. On the case. Working towards it, documenting it.
3. Oops. No, not yet completed (or started).
4. This is all too overwhelming. I Need help with this – fast.

Investing & Funding

To build a successful and sustainable business, securing funding and investment is vital. It can be challenging to cover the costs of essential business operations, such as research and development, marketing, and operational expenses, without sufficient capital. This is where securing funding can play a crucial role.

There are various sources of funding available to businesses, including venture capitalists, angel investors, crowdfunding, grants, loans, and government programs. Each funding source has its unique advantages and disadvantages, and it is important to research and understand each option before deciding which one is right for your business.

For instance, venture capitalists typically invest in high-growth businesses that have the potential to provide a significant return on investment. On the other hand, crowdfunding can be an effective way to raise capital for many people who are passionate about your business idea.

Furthermore, securing funding can help businesses implement sustainable practices, such as investing in renewable energy sources, reducing waste, or developing environmentally friendly products. Not only do these practices help to reduce the environmental impact of the business, but they can also appeal to consumers who prioritize sustainability.

Finally, funding can provide businesses with the necessary resources to expand their offerings and reach new markets. This can lead to increased revenue and profitability, which can ensure the long-term viability of the business.

To assist you in achieving your investment goals, AI can be a useful tool. AI can help you to research your industry, sector, or niche to identify new sales and marketing opportunities. Additionally, AI-powered chatbots can assist in answering potential investor questions and provide valuable insights into market trends and investment opportunities.

In conclusion, securing funding and investment is essential for building a sustainable business. With various funding options available and AI-assisted research tools at your disposal, businesses can find the necessary capital to grow and thrive while making a positive impact on the environment and society.

Each of the points below are split into 4 parts.

- **Challenge:** common issue or obstacle often faced by business owners
- **Fraserism:** a helpful hint, tip, quote, or suggestion to help you in overcoming a challenge.
- **Potential Prompt:** a question, task, and prompt to ask your preferred ai-powered VA.
- **Benefit:** The potential benefit of researching, documenting, executing, automating, and refining a task, process, procedure, or workflow that addresses the underlying challenge.

Challenge: **Lack of clarity and direction in the business**
Fraserism: It's important to document your model, vision, and strategy to have a clear direction for your business. This can include creating a business plan that outlines your goals, target market, and marketing strategy. By documenting your plans, you can also share them with potential investors or partners to show them that you have a solid plan in place.
Potential Prompt: How can I create a comprehensive business plan?
Benefit: By having a documented plan, you can ensure that everyone involved in your business is on the same page and working towards the same goals.
It can also make it easier to secure funding or partnerships.

Challenge: **Uncertainty about what will happen in the future**
Fraserism: It's important to have an exit strategy in place so that you know what you want to achieve with your business in the long term.

This can include options such as selling the business, going public, or passing it on to family members. By documenting your exit strategy, you can also make sure that you are working towards your end goal and not getting too caught up in short-term gains.

Potential Prompt: How can I create an exit strategy for my business?

Benefit: Having a clear exit strategy can help you make better decisions for your business and ensure that you are working towards a specific goal.

Challenge: **Uncertainty about the financial viability of the business**

Fraserism: It's important to prepare financial projections for your business, including cash flow, profit and loss, break-even analysis, and sales projections. This can help you understand the financial feasibility of your business and make informed decisions about investments or funding. By preparing projections, you can also identify potential areas of concern and adjust your business plan.

Potential Prompt: How can I create financial projections for my business?

Benefit: By preparing financial projections, you can make informed decisions about investments or funding and identify areas for improvement in your business plan.

Challenge: **Difficulty in securing funding for the business**

Fraserism: One option for securing funding for your business is to approach private investors. This can include friends and family members, as well as professional investors who are interested in supporting new businesses. By building relationships with potential investors and presenting a strong business plan, you can increase your chances of securing funding.

Potential Prompt: How can I identify potential private investors for my business?

Benefit: Securing funding from private investors can provide the capital needed to grow and expand your business.

Challenge: **Difficulty in securing funding for the business**

Fraserism: Another option for securing funding for your business is to approach business angels, who are typically wealthy individuals looking to invest in new businesses. By building relationships with potential investors and presenting a strong business plan, you can increase your chances of securing funding.

Potential Prompt: How can I find business angels who are interested in investing in my business?

Benefit: Securing funding from business angels can provide the capital needed to grow and expand your business, as well as access to valuable expertise and resources.

Challenge: **A lack of a well-structured management team**

Fraserism: It is recommended that you identify the key positions required for the success of the business and assemble a competent management team with the relevant skills and experience. Identifying skill gaps and investing in training and development can also improve the team's effectiveness.

Potential Prompt: "What are the key roles in your management team, and how have you identified the skill gaps within your team?"

Benefit: A well-structured management team can help drive business success, improve decision-making, and attract investors.

Challenge: **Lack of understanding of operational and marketing costs and profit margins**

Fraserism: You should track and analyze your cost per lead, cost per sale, and profit margins to gain insight into the health of your business. This information can help you identify areas for improvement, optimize your resources, and make informed decisions about pricing and revenue projections.

Potential Prompt: "How do you calculate your cost per lead, cost per sale, and profit margins, and what insights have you gained from this analysis?"

Benefit: Understanding your cost per lead, cost per sale, and profit margins can improve decision-making, inform pricing strategies, and help you maintain a healthy cash flow.

Challenge: **Overvaluing or undervaluing your business**

Fraserism: Conduct a thorough analysis of your business and the market to determine a fair market valuation. Consider factors such as your revenue, market size, competition, and growth potential. Seeking advice from industry experts and engaging in market research can also help inform your valuation.

Potential Prompt: "How have you determined the fair market value of your business, and what factors did you consider?"

Benefit: Establishing a fair market valuation can help attract investors, secure appropriate funding, and set realistic growth targets.

Challenge: **Failure to protect your business name, idea, and intellectual property**

Fraserism: Protect your business name, idea, and intellectual property through patents, trademarks, copyrights, and other legal protections. Seek legal advice to ensure your intellectual property is adequately protected and enforceable.

Potential Prompt: "What steps have you taken to protect your business name, idea, and intellectual property?"

Benefit: Protecting your business name, idea, and intellectual property can prevent infringement and legal disputes, increase the value of your business, and attract potential investors.

Challenge: **Inadequate reporting and financial systems**

Fraserism: Implement appropriate reporting and financial systems that provide accurate and timely financial information. Utilize tools such as accounting software and dashboards to monitor performance and make informed decisions.

Potential Prompt: "What reporting and financial systems do you have in place, and how do they help you monitor and analyze your business's financial performance?"

Benefit: Implementing appropriate reporting and financial systems can help inform decision-making, provide accurate financial projections, and make it easier to secure funding.

 Q. Do you have or require investment or funding for your business? Do you use AI to help you find and secure funding opportunities? Do you use AI to help you gain clarity, vision, and purpose to embrace, create and live your vision?

1. Yes. All done, planned, documented & included in our business plan.

2. On the case. Working towards it, documenting it.

3. Oops. No, not yet completed (or started).

4. This is all too overwhelming. I Need help with this – fast.

MySpace was a pioneering social media platform with a peak valuation of $12 billion in 2008 and over 1,600 employees. However, MySpace failed to keep up with the rise of Facebook and other social media platforms that offered more user-friendly interfaces, better privacy controls, and superior mobile integration. As a result, users gradually migrated to other platforms, and MySpace's user base declined rapidly. The company was eventually sold for a fraction of its former value.

Get AI-powered help to save time, money & stress to do the jobs you hate, don't have time for, or simply don't want to do.

Reduce costs, improve efficiency & ROI to achieve your goals & objectives. It's your business. you're in control. You make the decisions.

You decide what you want to achieve next.

Protecting Your Idea & Business

Protecting your business is like protecting your home. Just as you secure your home with locks and alarms, it's essential to safeguard your business assets and intellectual property from potential threats.

Securing your intellectual property, such as patents, trademarks, and copyrights, is crucial in protecting your unique ideas and products from being copied by competitors. This helps you maintain a competitive edge in the market and ensures that your hard work and creativity are rewarded.

Likewise, safeguarding your business assets, such as equipment, inventory, and real estate, is crucial to prevent theft and damage. This can involve implementing security measures, obtaining insurance coverage, and having contingency plans in place to handle emergencies.

Additionally, mitigating risks and preventing potential legal issues is an important aspect of protecting your business. This can involve having proper contracts in place to govern your business relationships, obtaining necessary licenses and permits, and ensuring compliance with relevant regulations and laws.

To help you protect your ideas and assets, AI can be a valuable tool. AI-powered software can help you monitor and identify potential IP infringements, analyze patent data, and conduct comprehensive trademark searches. Furthermore, AI-powered chatbots can assist in answering common legal questions and provide guidance on compliance issues.

In summary, protecting your business is essential for long-term success. Just as you take steps to secure your home, it's important to safeguard your intellectual property and business assets to prevent theft, mitigate risks, and ensure the sustainability of your enterprise. With AI-powered tools at your disposal, protecting your business has never been more accessible or efficient.

Each of the points below are split into 4 parts.

- **Challenge:** common issue or obstacle often faced by business owners
- **Fraserism:** a helpful hint, tip, quote, or suggestion to help you in overcoming a challenge.
- **Potential Prompt:** a question, task, and prompt to ask your preferred ai-powered VA.
- **Benefit:** The potential benefit of researching, documenting, executing, automating, and refining a task, process, procedure, or workflow that addresses the underlying challenge.

Challenge: **Have you protected your idea?**
Fraserism: It is important to protect your idea to prevent others from stealing or copying it. One way to do this is by obtaining a patent or trademark. You can also use non-disclosure agreements (NDAs) when sharing your idea with others to prevent them from using or disclosing it without your permission.
Potential Prompt: What steps can I take to protect my unique idea?
Benefit: By protecting your idea, you can ensure that you maintain a competitive advantage in the market and prevent others from profiting from your hard work.

Challenge: **Have you come up with a name for your idea or business?**
Fraserism: It is important to choose a unique and memorable name for your idea or business that is not already in use by another company. You can check for existing trademarks or registered business names to avoid potential legal issues.
Potential Prompt: How can I choose a name for my business that won't conflict with existing trademarks?
Benefit: By choosing a unique and memorable name for your business, you can build brand recognition and prevent potential legal issues that may arise from using a name that is already in use by another company.

Challenge: **Have you protected your name?**

Fraserism: Once you have chosen a name for your business, it is important to protect it by registering it as a trademark. This will prevent others from using a similar name and help to establish your brand identity.

Potential Prompt: How can I protect my business name from being used by others?

Benefit: By registering your business name as a trademark, you can establish your brand identity and prevent others from using a similar name, which can lead to brand confusion and lost revenue.

Challenge: **Have you documented and protected your tangible assets?**

Fraserism: It is important to document and protect your tangible assets, such as equipment, inventory, and real estate. This can involve implementing security measures, obtaining insurance coverage, and taking steps to prevent theft.

Potential Prompt: How can I protect my business equipment from theft or damage?

Benefit: By documenting and protecting your tangible assets, you can ensure that your business is able to continue operating even in the event of unexpected challenges or losses.

Challenge: **Have you documented and protected your intangible assets?**

Fraserism: In addition to tangible assets, it is important to document and protect your intangible assets, such as intellectual property, customer data, and proprietary information. This can involve using NDAs, implementing security measures, and obtaining legal protection for your intellectual property.

Potential Prompt: How can I protect my business's intellectual property from being stolen or copied by others?

Benefit: By protecting your intangible assets, you can ensure that your business is able to maintain a competitive advantage and prevent others from profiting from your hard work.

Challenge: **Have you protected yourself, your business, against IPR theft from staff?**

Fraserism: It is important to take steps to prevent intellectual property theft by employees, such as implementing confidentiality agreements and restricting access to sensitive information. Regularly monitoring employee activity and conducting background checks can also help to prevent theft.

Potential Prompt: How can I prevent employees from stealing my business's intellectual property?

Benefit: By taking steps to prevent intellectual property theft by employees, you can protect your business's intellectual property and prevent potential legal issues that may arise from theft.

Challenge: **competitors stealing and using your innovations**

Fraserism: Conduct a thorough patent search to determine the novelty of your invention, file a patent application with the appropriate intellectual property office, and work with an experienced patent attorney to ensure your patent application is robust and legally sound.

Potential Prompt: What steps should I take to apply for a patent registration for my invention?

Benefit: Securing a patent registration helps protect your intellectual property, strengthens your position in the marketplace, and can generate revenue through licensing agreements or the sale of your patented invention.

Challenge: **No copyright protection, others may use or reproduce your creative works**

Fraserism: File a copyright application with the relevant intellectual property office to secure legal protection for your creative works, including literary, artistic, and musical works, as well as software, databases, and website content.

Potential Prompt: How do I copyright my original artwork?

Benefit: Copyright protection helps ensure that your creative works are protected from infringement and enables you to control how they are used and distributed, potentially generating revenue through licensing agreements or sales.

Challenge: **staff may misuse, steal, or disclose your IP to unauthorized parties.**

Fraserism: Develop comprehensive policies and procedures for protecting intellectual property shared with staff, including confidentiality agreements, employee training, and regular monitoring and auditing of intellectual property usage.

Potential Prompt: How can I ensure that my employees understand and comply with my company's intellectual property policies?

Benefit: Protecting intellectual property shared with staff helps mitigate the risk of theft, misappropriation, or unauthorized use, enabling you to maintain your competitive edge and reputation in the marketplace.

Challenge: **strategic partners may misuse, steal, or disclose your IP to unauthorized parties.**

Fraserism: Develop formal agreements with partners that clearly define the scope and ownership of intellectual property shared between parties, including patents, trademarks, copyrights, and trade secrets.

Potential Prompt: What should I include in a formal agreement to protect my intellectual property when collaborating with a partner?

Benefit: Properly documenting and protecting intellectual property shared with partners can help prevent disputes, litigation, and other legal issues, and facilitate successful collaboration and innovation.

Challenge: **suppliers may misuse, steal, or disclose your IP to unauthorized parties.**

Fraserism: Develop formal agreements with suppliers that outline the ownership, permitted use, and confidentiality of intellectual property shared between parties, and establish procedures for monitoring and enforcing compliance with these agreements.

Potential Prompt: What steps should I take to protect my intellectual property when collaborating with suppliers?

Benefit: Documenting and protecting intellectual property shared with suppliers can help mitigate the risk of unauthorized use or disclosure, strengthen supplier relationships, and safeguard your competitive position in the marketplace.

Challenge: **customers may misuse, steal, or disclose your IP to unauthorized parties.**

Fraserism: Develop formal agreements with customers that define the permitted use, ownership, and confidentiality of intellectual property shared between parties, and establish procedures for monitoring and enforcing compliance with these agreements.

Potential Prompt: How can I protect my proprietary software when licensing it to customers?

Q. Have you protected your business idea and business assets? Do you use AI to help your document and protect systems, processes, and assets? Do you use AI to help you gain clarity, vision, and purpose to embrace, create and live your vision?

1. Yes. All done, planned, documented & included in our business plan.

2. On the case. Working towards it, documenting it.

3. Oops. No, not yet completed (or started).

4. This is all too overwhelming. I Need help with this – fast.

Definition

h@ppeneur® n. *an individual who plans, documents, executes & automates their marketing online to start and grow a business, achieve their personal goals in order to live the life and lifestyle they want.*

Definition

intr@preneur® n. *is an employee within a company who plans, documents, executes & automates their marketing online leveraging the organisation's resources to achieve their own personal goals <u>and</u> the corporate objectives.*

Branding

Branding is crucial for any business because it allows you to differentiate yourself from competitors and build a unique identity. A well-defined brand strategy helps to create trust and loyalty with customers, which can lead to increased sales and profits. Effective branding can also help to establish your business as an industry leader and attract top talent.

By creating a strong brand, businesses can better communicate their values and mission to their audience, helping to establish an emotional connection with their customers. This connection can lead to increased customer retention and referral rates, which can lead to greater success overall.

Additionally, a consistent brand message and visual identity can help to establish credibility with potential customers and clients, making it easier to close deals and win new business.

Overall, branding is a critical component of any successful business, helping to establish a clear and compelling identity, build customer loyalty, and drive long-term growth and profitability.

When it comes to your branding, you could use AI to help you with your brand promise, brand story and the rest of your branding. Here are a few suggestions to help address common branding challenges and how you can ask, prompt, or instruct AI to assist you in achieving your branding goals and objectives on time, within budget and without quibble.

Each of the points below are split into 4 parts.

- **Challenge:** common issue or obstacle often faced by business owners
- **Fraserism:** a helpful hint, tip, quote, or suggestion to help you in overcoming a challenge.
- **Potential Prompt:** a question, task, and prompt to ask your preferred ai-powered VA.

- **Benefit:** The potential benefit of researching, documenting, executing, automating, and refining a task, process, procedure, or workflow that addresses the underlying challenge.

Challenge: **debating whether it's worth the effort.**
Fraserism: A strong brand identity is essential for businesses to stand out in crowded markets, attract customers, and build loyalty. By defining your brand's unique value proposition, positioning, messaging, and visual identity, you can differentiate your business and communicate your value to customers.
Potential Prompt: What are some ways to define my brand's unique value proposition and differentiate my business from competitors?
Benefit: A strong brand identity can help your business establish a unique identity and build a loyal customer base, leading to increased revenue and market share.

Challenge: **it can be difficult to create a brand that stands out and engages customers.**
Fraserism: A strong brand that resonates with customers is built on a clear understanding of your target audience, their pain points, and what makes your business unique. By creating a compelling brand story, messaging, and visual identity that speaks directly to your audience's needs and emotions, you can differentiate your business and build a loyal following.
Potential Prompt: How can I create a brand story and messaging that resonates with my target audience and differentiates my business?
Benefit: An impactful and engaging brand can help you attract and retain customers, build trust and loyalty, and drive revenue and growth.

Challenge: **underestimate the role that branding plays in attracting and retaining customers**
Fraserism: A strong brand can create an emotional connection with customers and communicate your company's values, personality, and mission. By consistently delivering on your brand promise and building a relationship with your customers, you can create a loyal customer base that is more likely to recommend your business to others.

Potential Prompt: How can I use branding to build a relationship with my customers and increase loyalty?

Benefit: A strong brand can help you build a loyal customer base, leading to increased revenue and market share over time.

Challenge: **Maintaining a consistent brand message across all channels**

Fraserism: A consistent brand message and visual identity help to reinforce your brand's unique value proposition and increase brand awareness and recognition. By creating brand guidelines and training employees on how to communicate and represent your brand, you can ensure that your brand message is consistent and aligned across all touchpoints.

Potential Prompt: How can I ensure that my brand message is consistent across all channels and touchpoints?

Benefit: Consistent branding can increase brand awareness and recognition, leading to greater customer loyalty and revenue over time.

Challenge: **Businesses may not recognize the impact that branding has on customer loyalty**

Fraserism: A strong brand creates an impression on customers and can lead to repeat business and referrals. By creating a distinctive brand identity and delivering a consistent brand experience, you can create a memorable brand that stands out from competitors and resonates with customers.

Potential Prompt: How can I create a memorable brand that stands out from competitors and resonates with customers?

Benefit: A memorable brand can increase customer loyalty and repeat business, leading to increased revenue and market share over time.

Challenge: **confusion among customers and difficulty in standing out from competitors.**

Fraserism: Conduct a brand audit to evaluate your current branding efforts and identify areas for improvement. Define your brand values, mission statement, and brand voice to guide all future branding decisions. Develop a visual identity, including a logo and color palette, to create a cohesive brand image.

Potential Prompt: "How can I establish a clear and consistent brand identity for my business?"

Benefit: Establishing a clear and consistent brand identity can help increase brand recognition and loyalty among customers, leading to long-term business success.

Challenge: **Your branding efforts may result in a lack of relevance and effectiveness.**

Fraserism: Conduct market research to identify your target audience and tailor your branding efforts to their needs and preferences. Develop buyer personas to better understand your ideal customer and craft messaging that speaks directly to them.

Potential Prompt: "How can I ensure my branding efforts are targeted towards specific customer demographics?"

Benefit: Targeted branding can increase the effectiveness of your marketing efforts and help you better connect with your ideal customer, driving business growth.

Challenge: **You don't have a brand style guide**

Fraserism: Create a brand style guide that outlines your brand's visual elements, including color palettes, typography, and image styles. Use this guide to ensure all marketing materials, both online and offline, adhere to your brand's standards.

Potential Prompt: "How can I create a brand style guide to ensure consistency across all marketing materials?"

Benefit: A brand style guide can help maintain a consistent brand identity across all marketing materials, improving brand recognition and building trust with customers.

Challenge: **Not knowing whether your branding is resonating with your audience, leading**

Fraserism: Conduct market research, such as surveys, focus groups, and online analytics, to gather feedback on your branding efforts. Use this information to make data-driven decisions about your branding strategy.

Potential Prompt: "How can I conduct market research to determine the effectiveness of my branding efforts?"

Benefit: Conducting market research can provide valuable insights into your target audience's preferences and perceptions of your brand, allowing you to make informed decisions about your branding

115

strategy.

Challenge: **Not using branding to establish a strong company culture**
Fraserism: Develop a strong company culture that aligns with your brand values and mission. Foster a sense of community among employees and encourage them to embody your brand's personality and values in all customer interactions.
Potential Prompt: "How can I use branding to establish a strong company culture that aligns with my brand values?"
Benefit: A strong company culture that aligns with your brand values can improve employee morale and engagement, leading to better customer interactions and increased brand loyalty.

Challenge: **Not integrating your brand into product packaging and labeling**
Fraserism: Incorporate your brand's visual elements, such as logo and color palette, into your product packaging and labeling. Use consistent messaging and imagery to create a cohesive brand experience for customers.
Potential Prompt: "How can I integrate my brand into my product packaging and labeling?"
Benefit: Incorporating your brand into product packaging and labeling can increase brand recognition and improve customer loyalty by creating a cohesive brand experience.

 Q. Have you implemented a branding strategy for your business? Do you use AI to help your document and implement a branding strategy? Do you use AI to help you gain clarity, vision, and purpose to embrace, create and live your vision?

1. Yes. All done, planned, documented & included in our business plan.

2. On the case. Working towards it, documenting it.

3. Oops. No, not yet completed (or started).

4. This is all too overwhelming. I Need help with this – fast.

Human Resources

Starting and running a successful business is not just about having a great product or service, it's also about creating a positive work culture. Imagine if your business were a garden, the employees would be the flowers, and the work culture would be the soil. For the flowers to thrive and bloom, you need to have nutrient-rich soil that provides a favorable environment for growth. Similarly, a positive work culture can help employees flourish, stay engaged and committed to the business.

Creating a positive work culture means giving your employees a sense of purpose and belonging. It's about providing opportunities for growth and development, recognizing, and rewarding their hard work, and fostering open communication and collaboration. When employees feel valued, they are more likely to be motivated, engaged, and productive.

However, it's not just about creating a good work environment, businesses also need to comply with employment legislation to ensure fair treatment of employees. Think of employment legislation as the fence around your garden. It keeps things in order and ensures that everything is done in a fair and legal manner. By complying with employment legislation, businesses can avoid legal issues and protect their reputation.

Prioritizing human resources and culture is not just good for employees, it's good for business. When employees are happy, engaged, and productive, it leads to increased customer satisfaction, profitability, and a better reputation. It's like having a well-maintained garden that attracts visitors and admirers.

Ultimately, investing in human resources and culture is essential for sustained success in today's competitive marketplace. By creating a positive work environment and complying with employment legislation, businesses can attract top talent, retain employees, and achieve long-term success.

You could use AI to help you manage your team, your staff, sub-contractors, and suppliers by writing clear SOPs (standard operating procedures), policies, procedures, agreements, and contracts to protect them and you. Here are a few suggestions to help address common branding challenges and how you can ask, prompt, or instruct AI to assist you in achieving your branding goals and objectives on time, within budget and without quibble.

Each of the points below are split into 4 parts.

- **Challenge:** common issue or obstacle often faced by business owners
- **Fraserism:** a helpful hint, tip, quote, or suggestion to help you in overcoming a challenge.
- **Potential Prompt:** a question, task, and prompt to ask your preferred ai-powered VA.
- **Benefit:** The potential benefit of researching, documenting, executing, automating, and refining a task, process, procedure, or workflow that addresses the underlying challenge.

Challenge: **providing meaningful work for staff**
Fraserism: To provide meaningful work, consider aligning the job responsibilities and tasks with the interests and strengths of the employee. Provide opportunities for professional development and growth and encourage open communication to understand what motivates and drives each individual employee.
Potential Prompt: "How can we ensure that our employees are engaged and feel that their work is meaningful?"
Benefit: Providing meaningful work can increase employee satisfaction and motivation, leading to higher productivity and retention rates.

Challenge: **Hiring sub-contractors can be risky if proper due diligence is not taken,**

Fraserism: Before hiring subcontractors, thoroughly vet them and their credentials, and ensure that they have proper insurance and licensing. Draft a comprehensive contract that outlines the scope of work, timelines, payment terms, and liability provisions.

Potential Prompt: "What steps should we take before hiring a subcontractor to ensure that we are protected legally and financially?"

Benefit: Properly vetting and hiring sub-contractors can help ensure quality work, timely completion of projects, and mitigate the risk of legal and financial consequences.

Challenge: **Hiring casual or part-time labour**

Fraserism: Consider creating a clear and consistent schedule that outlines expectations for work hours and responsibilities and provides clear guidelines for communication and accountability. Consider hiring a staffing agency to help with managing scheduling and ensuring consistent quality of work.

Potential Prompt: "How can we manage schedules and ensure consistent quality of work when hiring casual or part-time labor?"

Benefit: Implementing clear guidelines and schedules can help ensure consistency and quality of work, while using a staffing agency can help with managing schedules and ensuring adequate coverage.

Challenge: **an organization chart**

Fraserism: Create an organization chart that outlines the hierarchy of roles and responsibilities within the organization and ensures that all employees have access to and understand the chart.

Potential Prompt: "What are the benefits of having an organization chart, and how can we create one for our business?"

Benefit: Having an organization chart can help clarify roles and responsibilities, improve communication and accountability, and ensure that everyone is working towards the same objectives.

Challenge: **a clear understanding of the roles and positions that need to be filled**

Fraserism: Conduct a thorough analysis of the business's needs and objectives and create a comprehensive list of the positions and roles that need to be filled. Create detailed job descriptions that outline the responsibilities, qualifications, and expectations for each position.

Potential Prompt: "How can we determine what positions and roles we need to fill in our business, and what should we include in job descriptions?"

Benefit: Having a clear understanding of the positions and roles that need to be filled can help ensure that the business has the necessary resources to meet its objectives, while detailed job descriptions can help attract and hire the right candidates.

Challenge: **Not keeping current with employment legislation**

Fraserism: Set up a system for regular reviews of employment legislation and assign someone to stay up to date with any changes. This could involve subscribing to industry newsletters or attending relevant training courses.

Potential Prompt: "What is your process for staying current with employment legislation?"

Benefit: By staying current with employment legislation, the business can avoid legal issues and potential financial penalties, which can save time and money in the long run.

Challenge: **Not offering bonuses, incentives, or share options**

Fraserism: Consider offering a variety of incentives, such as bonuses for achieving certain goals, share options for longer-term employees, or other benefits that align with your company culture and values.

Potential Prompt: "What types of incentives do you plan to offer your staff?"

Benefit: Offering incentives can help to boost staff morale and motivation, leading to increased productivity and potentially lower staff turnover.

Challenge: Not clearly defining roles, responsibilities, and resources can lead to confusion and inefficiencies within the team.

Fraserism: Clearly define each employee's role, responsibilities, and resources necessary to perform their job effectively. This could involve creating detailed job descriptions, setting performance metrics, and providing necessary training and resources.

Potential Prompt: "How have you defined the roles, responsibilities, and resources for your staff?"

Benefit: Clear definitions of roles, responsibilities, and resources can help to ensure that each employee understands their job and can perform effectively, leading to increased productivity and potentially higher job satisfaction.

Challenge: **Not budgeting for staff**

Fraserism: Create a detailed budget for staffing, including salaries, benefits, and other associated costs. Consider a range of scenarios, including best and worst case, to ensure that the budget is realistic and sustainable.

Potential Prompt: "Have you created a budget for your staffing needs?"

Benefit: Creating a realistic and sustainable staffing budget can help to ensure that the business has the necessary resources to support its employees, leading to increased productivity and potentially lower staff turnover.

Challenge: **applying for government grants and financial assistance**

Fraserism: Research and identify any government financial assistance programs that may be available for hiring staff. This could include tax incentives, training grants, or other subsidies.

Potential Prompt: "Have you researched any government financial assistance programs for hiring staff?"

Benefit: Qualifying for government financial assistance can help to offset the costs of hiring staff, potentially saving the business money, and increasing its competitiveness.

Challenge: **Not having a pension scheme in place**

Fraserism: Set up a pension scheme for your employees and consider matching their contributions to incentivize participation.

Potential Prompt: "Do you have a pension scheme in place for your employees?"

Benefit: Offering a pension scheme can help to attract and retain employees, leading to a more stable and motivated workforce.

Challenge: **staff expenses**

Fraserism: Set up a clear system for addressing and approving staff expenses and provide clear guidelines for what types of expenses are covered and how to submit them.

Potential Prompt: "How do you manage staff expenses?"

Benefit: Having a clear system for handling staff expenses can help to avoid confusion and ensure that the business is only paying for necessary and approved expenses.

Q. Have you implemented a branding strategy for your business? Do you use AI to help your document and implement a branding strategy? Do you use AI to help you gain clarity, vision, and purpose to embrace, create and live your vision?

1. Yes. All done, planned, documented & included in our business plan.
2. On the case. Working towards it, documenting it.
3. Oops. No, not yet completed (or started).
4. This is all too overwhelming. I Need help with this – fast.

Legal Considerations

It's important to have a clear understanding of the legal requirements for starting and operating a business. This includes registering your business, obtaining necessary licenses and permits, and complying with relevant regulations and legislation. Failure to do so can result in penalties and legal consequences that can harm your business.

Additionally, creating policies and documents such as contracts, terms and conditions, and privacy policies can provide essential protection for your business and its customers. These documents outline your obligations and responsibilities and help prevent disputes and legal issues. Adequate insurance coverage is also crucial for protecting your business from unexpected events and liabilities.

Furthermore, compliance with data protection laws and regulations, such as GDPR and CCPA, is essential for protecting customer data and maintaining their trust. Failing to comply with these regulations can result in significant fines and damage to your business reputation.

Whether it's protecting your idea, your premises, yourself, or your staff or whether it's complying with local, national, or international law, starting a business involves navigating complex legal requirements and implementing policies, documents, agreements, and compliance measures. There can also be specific requirements and compliance to be performed in your industry, sector or niche and bodies like www.FSB.org.uk can help. Ensuring you understand and meet all these requirements is essential for protecting you, your staff, your business, and its customers and avoiding potential legal consequences. Seek expert advice and support to ensure you cover all necessary aspects and safeguard your business's success.

Having said that, you could use AI to help you consider potential wording in agreements, policies, contracts, and SOPs to assist you in complying with key regulations. You can ask AI to assist you in creating your own procedures, agreements, and contracts to protect you. However, I do recommend that you do seek independent legal advice for maximum protection. Legislation is always changing, and AI can and does sometimes get things wrong. It's great in helping you to do a lot of the heavy lifting and saving you valuable time and to help you gain clarity on a situation and in deciding a course of action.

Here are a few suggestions to help address common branding challenges and how you can ask, prompt, or instruct AI to assist you in achieving your branding goals and objectives on time, within budget and without quibble.

Each of the points below are split into 4 parts.

- **Challenge:** common issue or obstacle often faced by business owners
- **Fraserism:** a helpful hint, tip, quote, or suggestion to help you in overcoming a challenge.
- **Potential Prompt:** a question, task, and prompt to ask your preferred ai-powered VA.
- **Benefit:** The potential benefit of researching, documenting, executing, automating, and refining a task, process, procedure, or workflow that addresses the underlying challenge.

Challenge: **understanding the different types of business structures**
Fraserism: Seek expert advice to determine the most appropriate business structure based on your specific needs and circumstances. Consider factors such as liability, taxation, and ownership when making your decision.
Potential Prompt: "Can you explain the different types of business structures available, and which one would be most suitable for my business?"
Benefit: By choosing the appropriate business structure, you can protect your personal assets, reduce your tax liability, and ensure compliance with legal requirements.

Challenge: **Register for VAT, NI, and taxation purposes c**

Fraserism: Register for VAT, NI, and taxation purposes as required by law. Seek expert advice to ensure you complete the process correctly and comply with all legal requirements.

Potential Prompt: "What is the process for registering for VAT, NI, and taxation purposes, and what are the consequences of not registering?"

Benefit: Registering for VAT, NI, and taxation purposes enables your business to operate legally, claim back VAT on business expenses, and avoid penalties for non-compliance.

Challenge: **registering and protecting your business name**

Fraserism: Register your business name and other relevant assets, such as trademarks and patents, to protect them from infringement and misuse. Seek expert advice to ensure you complete the process correctly and comply with all legal requirements. Also check out www.start.biz.

Potential Prompt: "How can I register and protect my business name and other relevant assets, and why is it important?"

Benefit: Registering and protecting your business name and other relevant assets can increase your business's value, protect your intellectual property, and prevent legal disputes.

Challenge: **Failing to meet all the necessary legal requirements for stationery**

Fraserism: Ensure your stationery meets all necessary legal requirements, such as including your business name, registered address, and company registration number. Seek expert advice to ensure compliance with all relevant legislation.

Potential Prompt: "What are the necessary legal requirements for stationery, and how can I ensure compliance?"

Benefit: Meeting all necessary legal requirements for stationery can increase your business's credibility, comply with legal requirements, and avoid legal disputes.

Challenge: **Failing to meet all the necessary legal requirements for your website**

Fraserism: Ensure your website meets all necessary legal requirements, such as privacy policies, terms and conditions, and cookie notices. Seek expert advice to ensure compliance with all relevant legislation.

Potential Prompt: "What are the necessary legal requirements for a website, and how can I ensure compliance?"

Benefit: Meeting all necessary legal requirements for your website can increase your business's credibility, comply with legal requirements, and avoid legal disputes.

Challenge: **health & safety requirements**

Fraserism: It's crucial to protect your business and employees by ensuring that you comply with all health and safety regulations. A suggestion is to conduct a risk assessment to identify any hazards in the workplace and take appropriate steps to eliminate or control those risks. You should also provide adequate training for employees on health and safety matters and have proper policies and procedures in place to address any incidents or accidents that may occur.

Potential Prompt: What are the necessary steps I need to take to ensure my business complies with all health and safety regulations?

Benefit: By taking these steps, you can prevent workplace accidents and illnesses, which can result in significant costs to your business, such as legal claims, compensation payments, and reputational damage.

Challenge: **selling or buying online**

Fraserism: If you plan to sell or buy online, it's essential to protect yourself by creating clear terms and conditions for your website or platform. This includes outlining payment and delivery terms, refund policies, and any other important details that users need to be aware of before they make a purchase. You should also have appropriate legal agreements in place with any third-party vendors or suppliers that you work with, and make sure that you comply with data protection and consumer protection regulations.

Potential Prompt: What legal documents do I need to protect myself when selling goods or services online?

Benefit: By having clear terms and conditions and appropriate legal agreements in place, you can reduce the risk of disputes and legal claims arising from online transactions.

Challenge: **Not having an accountant**

Fraserism: It's important to have an accountant review your business plan. and projected legal costs to ensure that you have a realistic budget in place and that you are not underestimating the costs of legal compliance. They can also provide guidance on tax planning and financial management to help your business succeed.

Potential Prompt: What are the benefits of having an accountant review my business plan and projected legal costs?

Benefit: By having an accountant review your financial plans and legal costs, you can gain valuable insights and advice on how to manage your finances effectively and avoid costly mistakes.

Challenge: **Finding the money to pay for legal advice**

Fraserism: It's important to check whether your insurance policies include any free legal advice or support services, (also sites like www.fsb.org.uk) as this can be a valuable resource if you need help with legal matters. For example, some policies may offer access to legal helplines or online legal documents.

Potential Prompt: Are there any free legal advice or support services included in my insurance policies?

Benefit: By taking advantage of free legal advice or support services, you can access professional legal guidance without incurring additional costs, which can be particularly helpful for small businesses with limited budgets.

Challenge: **"late payments"**

Fraserism: Late payments can cause significant cash flow problems for businesses, so it's important to have clear payment terms, clear credit terms (if you offer them) and follow-up procedures in place. This includes setting out clear payment deadlines and penalties for late payments, as well as having appropriate debt recovery procedures in place if necessary.

Potential Prompt: What steps can I take to protect myself against late payments from customers or clients?

Benefit: By protecting yourself against late payments, you can reduce the risk of cash flow problems and ensure that your business has the necessary funds to operate effectively.

Q. Have you considered all the legal implications for your business? Do you use AI to help you document and implement a legal strategy? Do you use AI to help you gain clarity, vision, and purpose to embrace, create and live your vision?

1. Yes. All done, planned, documented & included in our business plan.
2. On the case. Working towards it, documenting it.
3. Oops. No, not yet completed (or started).
4. This is all too overwhelming. I Need help with this – fast.

AI & MarTech

People are stressed, searching for fulfillment from meaningful work as managers, owners, stakeholders and shareholders and investors become more demanding in wanting more and more for less and less. This inevitably can take its toll on a person's demeanour, personality, enthusiasm, and health. This can undoubtedly have a dramatic impact on the health of the business if key processes, workflow, and SOPs (standard operating procedures) are not streamlined and made more efficient.

Harnessing the power of AI, MarTech, and technology in business is essential in today's fast-paced and highly competitive world. These technological advancements provide businesses with the ability to save time, money and reduce stress for all concerned.

Using AI and machine learning algorithms, businesses can automate repetitive and mundane tasks, freeing up employees to focus on more important and strategic activities. This not only saves time but also allows for better resource allocation, resulting in cost savings for the organization.

MarTech tools such as customer relationship management (CRM) systems, social media management platforms, and email marketing software help businesses improve their communication and engagement with customers. By using MarTech tools, businesses can deliver personalized content and offers to customers at scale, improving customer satisfaction and retention.

Furthermore, technology provides businesses with access to real-time data and insights, enabling them to make informed decisions quickly. This can help reduce stress by reducing the uncertainty that comes with making critical business decisions.

In conclusion, harnessing the power of AI, MarTech, and technology is crucial for businesses looking to remain competitive in today's market. By leveraging these tools, businesses can save time, reduce costs, and make informed decisions, leading to increased efficiency and success. Here are a few suggestions to help address common branding challenges and how you can ask, prompt, or instruct AI to assist you in achieving your branding goals and objectives on time, within budget and without quibble.

Each of the points below are split into 4 parts.

- **Challenge:** common issue or obstacle often faced by business owners
- **Fraserism:** a helpful hint, tip, quote, or suggestion to help you in overcoming a challenge.
- **Potential Prompt:** a question, task, and prompt to ask your preferred ai-powered VA.
- **Benefit:** The potential benefit of researching, documenting, executing, automating, and refining a task, process, procedure, or workflow that addresses the underlying challenge.

Challenge: **not be aware of what tools and platforms are essential in a martech stack.**
Fraserism: You should research the essential tools and platforms for a martech stack and identify which ones are most relevant to your business needs, and check out www.itstacksup.com
Potential Prompt: What are the essential tools and platforms for a martech stack and how can I choose the right ones for my business?
Benefit: Building an effective martech stack can help you streamline your marketing and sales processes, improve customer experiences, and drive growth for your business.
Do you have automated accounting, sales process, and customer journey?

Challenge: **spending too much time on manual processes and procedures**
Fraserism: You should implement automation tools for these processes to save time and increase efficiency to allow you to free up your time and spend more quality time with your family.
Potential Prompt: What are some automation tools that I can use to

streamline my accounting, sales, and customer journey processes?
Benefit: Implementing automation tools can help you save time, reduce errors, and increase productivity in your business operations.

Challenge: **You may not be generating enough leads or traffic to your website**
Fraserism: You should research, identify effective lead sources, and traffic sources that are relevant to your target audience and industry. We can specifically help with this on our website.
Potential Prompt: What are some effective lead and traffic sources that I can use to increase growth and revenue for my business?
Benefit: Having excellent lead and traffic sources can help you increase brand awareness, generate more leads, and drive more revenue for your business.

Challenge: **using personal versions of software that may not have the features for your needs**
Fraserism: You should ensure that you are using business versions of software that are tailored to your business needs and have all the necessary features and capabilities.
Potential Prompt: How can I ensure that I am using business versions of software that are tailored to my business needs and have all the necessary features and capabilities?
Benefit: Using business versions of software can help you improve efficiency, productivity, and collaboration among team members.

Challenge: **Your Internet Connection (or phone provider)**
Fraserism: You should research and identify the type of internet connection that is most suitable for your business needs. You can also use an excellent free tool – www.speedtest.net
Potential Prompt: What type of internet connection is most suitable for my business needs and how can I ensure that I have the necessary bandwidth and speed?
Benefit: Having the right type of internet connection can help you improve productivity, efficiency, and collaboration among team members.

Challenge: **managing people, tasks, and projects efficiently.**
Fraserism: Consider using a cloud-based task manager such as Trello,

Asana, or Monday.com to manage your tasks, projects, and teams. These tools allow you to collaborate with team members in real-time, set deadlines, track progress, and prioritize tasks.

Potential Prompt: What cloud-based task manager do you recommend for managing projects and teams?

Benefit: Using a cloud-based task manager can help you streamline your workflow, increase productivity, and ensure everyone is on the same page.

Challenge: **Storing data locally can be risky as it can be lost due to hardware failure**

Fraserism: Consider storing your data in the cloud using services such as Dropbox, Google Drive, or Microsoft OneDrive. These cloud storage solutions provide backup and synchronization of your data across multiple devices, allowing you to access your files from anywhere.

Potential Prompt: How can I ensure my data is secure and accessible from anywhere?

Benefit: Storing your data in the cloud provides a secure backup and allows you to access your files from anywhere, ensuring that your data is always available when you need it.

Challenge: **Not using APIs to link and connect more efficient tools and software**

Fraserism: Consider using APIs (application programming interfaces) to connect different software and website solutions into one. APIs allow you to automate data entry, streamline workflows, and reduce errors.

Potential Prompt: How can I connect different software solutions into one?

Benefit: Using APIs can help you automate tasks, reduce errors, and increase efficiency, saving you time and money.

Challenge: **Not synchronizing your laptop/PC with your smartphone or cloud-based solutions**

Fraserism: Use cloud-based solutions such as Google Drive, OneDrive, or iCloud to synchronize your files and notifications across devices. This ensures that you have access to your data and notifications on all your devices, even when you're on the go.

Potential Prompt: How can I synchronize my laptop and smartphone to avoid data loss and missed notifications?

Benefit: Synchronizing your devices ensures that you have access to your data and notifications on all your devices, increasing productivity and reducing the risk of data loss.

Challenge: **Managing accounting data manually**

Fraserism: Use cloud-based accounting software such as QuickBooks, Xero, or FreshBooks to manage your accounting data. These tools provide automation, invoicing, and financial reporting features, making accounting easy and hassle-free.

Potential Prompt: What cloud-based accounting software do you recommend?

Benefit: Using cloud-based accounting software can help you manage your finances more efficiently, reduce errors, and save you time.

Challenge: **Not automating and personalizing the customer journey,**

Fraserism: Use customer relationship management (CRM) software such as HubSpot, Salesforce, itstacksup.com or Zoho to automate and personalize the customer journey. These tools provide features such as lead tracking, personalized email campaigns, and customer analytics, making it easier to provide an excellent customer experience.

Potential Prompt: How can I automate and personalize the customer journey?

Benefit: Automating and personalizing the customer journey can help you provide an exceptional customer experience, improve customer retention, and increase revenue.

 Q. Have you considered all ai, martech or technology for your business? Do you use AI to help you streamline tasks, procedures, and workflows to save you time, money & stress? Do you use AI to help you gain clarity, vision, and purpose to embrace, create and live your vision?

1. Yes. All done, planned, documented & I have a martech stack in place.

2. **On the case. Working towards it, documenting it.**

3. **Oops. No, not yet completed (or started).**

4. **This is all too overwhelming. I Need help with this – fast.**

Yahoo! was a major internet company with a peak revenue of $7.2 billion in 2008 and over 12,000 employees. However, Yahoo! failed to keep up with the rise of social media and the shift towards personalized content experiences.

Competitors like Google and Facebook were able to offer more advanced search algorithms and better targeted advertising. Yahoo! also faced competition from specialized online services like Twitter and LinkedIn. Despite attempts to diversify its business and expand into new markets, Yahoo! was unable to keep up and was eventually acquired by Verizon Communications in 2017.

Get AI-powered help to save time, money & stress to do the jobs you hate, don't have time for, or simply don't want to do.

Reduce costs, improve efficiency & ROI to achieve your goals & objectives. It's your business. you're in control. You make the decisions.

You decide what you want to achieve next.

Start-up Costs

Starting a business is an exciting but challenging venture that requires careful planning and financial management. One of the most important aspects of starting a business is to confirm your start-up costs and the required investment. Working from home can indeed help to reduce costs, and since the Covid-19 pandemic, thousands have opted to leave corporate life and start a business working from home.

You need to understand and cost out all the financial requirements of your business and ensure that you have enough resources to launch and sustain your venture in that all important first year of business (and beyond).

Start-up costs may include expenses such as equipment, office or retail space, inventory, marketing, and legal fees. By confirming your start-up costs, you can develop a realistic budget and avoid overspending, which can be detrimental to your business's success.

If you need to raise investment for your business, it's important to have a solid understanding of how much capital you require and for what you will use it. You can approach investors with a well-defined business plan that clearly outlines your financial projections and expected return on investment.

In addition to confirming your start-up costs, it's crucial to keep your costs down when starting a business. This involves being resourceful and finding ways to save money without sacrificing quality or customer experience. For instance, you may consider operating from a virtual office or shared workspace instead of renting a traditional office space or outsourcing certain tasks to freelancers or contractors rather than hiring full-time employees.

By keeping your costs down, you can reduce your financial risk and increase your chances of success. With careful planning and management, you can launch a successful business that is financially stable and poised for growth.

Quite often, you can start a business without needing a bank loan, overdraft, angel, or investor funding simply by leveraging your social networks and securing sales. If you've done your costing correctly, chances are you don't need that many sales to start generating a profit and cover all your costs.

How much are 1, 5 or 12 new customers worth to you? □

Each of the points below are split into 4 parts.

- **Challenge:** common issue or obstacle often faced by business owners
- **Fraserism:** a helpful hint, tip, quote, or suggestion to help you in overcoming a challenge.
- **Potential Prompt:** a question, task, and prompt to ask your preferred ai-powered VA.
- **Benefit:** The potential benefit of researching, documenting, executing, automating, and refining a task, process, procedure, or workflow that addresses the underlying challenge.

Challenge: **Not investing in professional, technical, and marketing support**
Fraserism: Do thorough research on the current market rates for professional, technical, and marketing services, and evaluate your business needs to determine how much you need to invest in each area. Also, consider the cost and benefit of various marketing channels to determine how much you need to invest in martech, sales, and marketing. Make a list of priorities and allocate a budget for each area accordingly. You could also explore what's inside itstacksup.com.
Potential Prompt: What is your strategy for determining the appropriate investment in professional, technical, and marketing support, as well as martech, sales, and marketing for your business?
Benefit: Knowing how much to invest in different areas of your business can help you make informed decisions, allocate resources effectively, and avoid overspending, which can improve your business's financial stability and growth potential.

Challenge: **keep costs down to avoid running out of funds too quickly.**

Fraserism: Look for opportunities to save money, such as using eBay or Amazon to purchase office supplies or equipment, or sourcing products from charity shops if appropriate for your business. However, don't sacrifice quality for price, and always compare the cost and benefits of various options before deciding.

Potential Prompt: Have you explored any cost-saving measures, such as using eBay or Amazon, or sourcing products from charity shops, to help keep your business expenses down?

Benefit: Keeping costs down can help you conserve resources, stay within budget, and increase your business's chances of success by ensuring you have enough funds to cover all your expenses, including unexpected ones.

Challenge: **not be able to secure enough funding to get it off the ground.**

Fraserism: To determine how much capital you need to start your business; you should create a detailed business plan that includes projected expenses and revenue. You should research the costs associated with starting similar businesses, and factor in expenses like rent, utilities, marketing, and equipment. You may also want to consult with a financial advisor to get a more accurate estimate.

Potential Prompt: How can I determine how much capital I need to start my business?

Benefit: Knowing how much capital you need will allow you to secure funding more easily and ensure that you have enough money to cover expenses during the start-up phase.

Challenge: **the costs involved in getting each revenue stream up and running.**

Fraserism: To determine how much it will cost to create and launch each revenue stream, you should create a detailed budget that includes all the associated expenses. This might include the cost of materials, labor, marketing, and other expenses. You should also research the prices of similar products or services to ensure that you are pricing your offerings competitively.

Potential Prompt: How can I determine how much it will cost to create and launch a new revenue stream?

Benefit: Knowing how much it will cost to create and launch each revenue stream will allow you to price your products or services accurately and maximize your revenue.

Challenge: **Not knowing your monthly incomings and outgoings**
Fraserism: To determine your monthly incomings and outgoings, you should keep detailed records of all your business transactions. You may also want to use accounting software to help you track your finances. By understanding your cash flow, you can make informed decisions about investments, expenses, and other financial matters. Also re-read the previous section on "your financial situation."
Potential Prompt: How can I keep track of my monthly incomings and outgoings?
Benefit: Knowing your monthly incomings and outgoings will allow you to manage your cash flow more effectively and make informed financial decisions.

Challenge: **simply not knowing what start-up costs you need**
Fraserism: To determine what start-up costs you need; you should create a detailed business plan that includes projected expenses and revenue. You should research the costs associated with starting similar businesses, and factor in expenses like rent, utilities, marketing, and equipment. You may also want to consult with a financial advisor to get a more accurate estimate. We also have a tool suite on the website called "The 90 Minute Business Plan".
Potential Prompt: How can I determine what start-up costs I need to become self-employed or start my business?
Benefit: Knowing what start-up costs you need will allow you to accurately budget for the launch of your business and ensure that you have enough money to cover expenses during the start-up phase.

Challenge: **not knowing your monthly overheads**
Fraserism: To determine your monthly overheads, you should create a detailed budget that includes all your ongoing expenses. This might include rent, utilities, salaries, marketing, and other expenses. You should also keep track of your expenses on an ongoing basis to ensure that you are staying within your budget. I offer a template budget in the "90 Minute Business Plan."
Potential Prompt: How can I determine my monthly overheads?

Benefit: Knowing your monthly overheads will allow you to accurately budget for ongoing expenses and ensure that you have enough money to cover your expenses each month.

Challenge: **No cashflow projections**
Fraserism: Research and create projections for your business, including cash flow, sales, balance sheet, break-even or profit and loss. This will help you better understand how your business will perform over time and allow you to make strategic decisions based on this information.
Potential Prompt: What is the projected cash flow, sales, and profit for my business for the next three years?
Benefit: Having projections in place can help you avoid financial surprises and make better-informed decisions regarding your business operations.

Challenge: **not understanding your potential ROI to attract investors or secure loans.**
Fraserism: Research and calculate your potential ROI to determine what you can offer investors or lenders as a repayment option. This will help you better understand how to structure your funding and investment strategy.
Potential Prompt: What ROI can my business offer potential investors or lenders?
Benefit: Knowing your ROI can help you better communicate your business's value and potential for growth to potential investors or lenders, increasing your chances of securing funding.

Challenge: **Errors in your business plan or financial data**
Fraserism: Hire an accountant to review your business plan and financial data to ensure accuracy and identify any potential issues. This will help you better understand the financial health of your business and identify areas for improvement.
Potential Prompt: Can an accountant review my business plan and financial data for accuracy?
Benefit: Having an accountant review your business plan and financial data can help you avoid costly mistakes and ensure the overall health of your business.

Challenge: **unable to set pricing and marketing strategies that are sustainable.**

Fraserism: Research and calculate your costs to determine what you can afford to pay for a sale or lead. This will help you better understand how to structure your pricing and marketing strategies to maximize profitability.

Potential Prompt: What are my costs for a sale and for a lead, and how can I use this information to set my pricing and marketing strategies?

Benefit: Understanding your costs can help you make better-informed decisions regarding your pricing and marketing strategies, increasing your profitability.

Challenge: **traditional Funding sources may not be available or viable.**

Fraserism: Research and investigate "soft loans" or government loans and crowd funding to determine if they are a viable funding option for your business. This can help you secure funding at a lower cost and with more favorable terms.

Potential Prompt: Are there any "soft loans" or government loans available for my business, and how can I apply for them?

Benefit: Investigating alternative funding options can help you secure funding at a lower cost and with more favorable terms, improving your business's financial health.

Challenge: **In addition to costs, not knowing what pricing and fees to charge**

Fraserism: Research and calculate your costs, fees, and potential revenue to determine what your pricing, or daily/hourly fees should be. This will help you set pricing that is sustainable and maximizes profitability. Remember your time, more importantly – opportunity cost in not acting or in reducing the time it takes to do something, can have a tremendous impact on your bottom line.

Potential Prompt: What should my pricing or daily/hourly fees be based on my costs and potential revenue?

Benefit: Calculating your pricing and potential discounting strategy can help to improve margins, and ROI for each revenue stream. Try and add or subtract value instead of discounting where possible.

Q. Are you generating enough leads for your products, services, and solutions? Do you use AI to help you to generate traffic, signups & registrations? Do you use AI to help you gain clarity, vision, and purpose to embrace, create and live your vision?

1. Yes. All done, planned, documented & implanted to generate leads.
2. On the case. Working towards it, documenting it.
3. Oops. No, not yet completed (or started).
4. This is all too overwhelming. I Need help with this – fast.

Time Management

Effective time management is crucial for the success of any business. By automating key tasks, processes, and workflows, businesses can save time and increase efficiency. This allows businesses to focus on important tasks that require human expertise, such as customer engagement and business strategy.

Automation can be implemented in various areas such as sales, marketing, finance, and operations. For example, businesses can automate their email marketing campaigns, social media posts, financial reports, and inventory management. This not only saves time, but also reduces the risk of errors and improves the overall quality of work.

By implementing automation, businesses can also reduce their operating costs and increase their profitability. Additionally, automation can help businesses stay competitive in today's fast-paced market, as they can respond quickly to market changes and customer needs.

So, time management and automation are critical for the success of any business. By streamlining tasks, businesses can save time, increase efficiency, reduce costs, and stay competitive. By embracing AI to the jobs, you hate, don't have time for simply don't want to do, can help improve your work life balance and contribute to a positive work culture.

Q. What are the jobs you hate, don't have time for or simply don't want to do? ☐

Each of the points below are split into 4 parts.

- **Challenge:** common issue or obstacle often faced by business owners
- **Fraserism:** a helpful hint, tip, quote, or suggestion to help you in overcoming a challenge.

- **Potential Prompt:** a question, task, and prompt to ask your preferred ai-powered VA.
- **Benefit:** The potential benefit of researching, documenting, executing, automating, and refining a task, process, procedure, or workflow that addresses the underlying challenge.

Challenge: **Do you know how many hours you spend a week online?**

Fraserism: Use a time-tracking tool to monitor your online activity and set limits on non-work-related browsing. For example, you can use the Rescue Time app to track the amount of time spent on different websites and apps.

Prompt: "What are some tools that can help me track my online activity and improve my productivity?"

Benefit: You can identify your time-wasting habits and work towards increasing your productivity.

Challenge: **Do you know how many hours you spend a week drafting documents & emails**

Fraserism: Use email templates and automation tools to streamline your communication process. Tools such as Mailchimp can help automate email marketing campaigns and manage subscriber lists.

Prompt: "How can I automate my email communication process to save time?"

Benefit: You can save time on repetitive tasks and focus on more important aspects of your business.

Challenge: **Do you know how many hours you spend a week on the phone?**

Fraserism: Use call tracking and automation tools to manage your incoming and outgoing calls. For example, you can use tools like Air call to track call analytics, manage call routing, and automate voicemail responses.

Prompt: "What are some tools that can help me manage my business calls more efficiently?"

Benefit: You can improve your customer service by ensuring that all calls are managed efficiently and effectively.

Challenge: **Do you know how many hours you spend a week on appointments?**
Fraserism: Use scheduling tools to automate your appointment booking process. For example, tools like Calendly can help schedule appointments, send reminders, and even integrate with other apps such as Zoom.
Prompt: "How can I streamline my appointment scheduling process?"
Benefit: You can save time on scheduling and focus on more important business tasks.

Challenge: **Do you know how many hours you spend a week at networking events?**
Fraserism: Use online networking tools to connect with others in your industry. For example, tools like LinkedIn can help you build relationships, share content, and even generate leads.
Prompt: "What are some online networking tools that can help me connect with others in my industry?"
Benefit: You can expand your network and generate more business opportunities.

Challenge: **Do you know your cost or rate per hour?**
Fraserism: Calculate your hourly rate based on your expenses and revenue goals. This can help you determine the value of your time and make better pricing decisions.
Prompt: "How can I calculate my hourly rate for my business?"
Benefit: You can ensure that your prices are fair and profitable.

Challenge: **Do you know how much of your time per week is spent researching?**
Fraserism: Use research tools and resources to help you find information more quickly. For example, tools like Google Scholar can help you find academic sources, while industry-specific databases can help you find relevant news and trends.
Prompt: "What are some research tools and resources that can help me find information more efficiently?"
Benefit: You can save time on research and make better-informed decisions.

Challenge: **Do you know how much of your time per week is spent planning?**
Fraserism: Use project management tools to help you plan and organize your tasks. For example, tools like Trello can help you create task lists, assign deadlines, and track progress.
Prompt: "What are some project management tools that can help me plan and organize my business tasks?"
Benefit: You can ensure that your projects are completed on time and within budget

Challenge: **No clear goals and objectives**
Fraserism: Yes, setting clear goals and objectives at all levels helps to provide direction and focus, ensuring that time and effort are allocated effectively. For example, I could set an annual goal to increase revenue by 20%, a quarterly goal to launch a new product, a monthly goal to improve customer retention, a weekly goal to complete a project milestone, and a daily goal to make 5 sales calls.
Potential Prompt: "What specific annual, quarterly, monthly, weekly, and daily goals should I consider in my life, career and business?"
Benefit: Setting clear goals and objectives helps to ensure that time and effort are spent on the most important tasks, allowing for better productivity and focus.

Challenge: **No todo or done list**
Fraserism: No, prioritising tasks is crucial for effective time management. Creating a to-do list and prioritising tasks based on importance and urgency can help to focus on the most important tasks and complete them efficiently. For example, I could use a tool like Trello or Asana to create a list of tasks and prioritize them based on importance and deadline.
Potential Prompt: "How do you prioritize your daily tasks to ensure you are completing the most important ones first?"
Benefit: Prioritising tasks helps to ensure that important tasks are completed efficiently, leading to increased productivity and reduced stress.

Challenge: **No daily, weekly, or monthly review**
Fraserism: No, reviewing progress and updating goals and to-do lists regularly is crucial for effective time management. Reviewing

progress at the end of each day and updating goals and to-do lists for the next day can help to stay on track and adjust priorities as needed. For example, I could set aside 10-15 minutes at the end of each day to review progress and update my to-do list for the next day.

Potential Prompt: "How often do you review your progress and update your goals and to-do list?"

Benefit: Regular review of progress and goals helps to ensure that time and effort are spent on the most important tasks, leading to increased productivity and success.

Challenge: **Trying to do everything yourself.**

Fraserism: Delegating, sub-contracting, or automating financial and admin tasks can help to save time and allow more focus on other important tasks. Setting deadlines for these tasks can help to ensure they are completed efficiently. For example, I could delegate bookkeeping tasks to a professional accountant, automate invoicing using software like QuickBooks or Xero, and set deadlines for vat returns, self-assessment completion and other financial tasks.

Potential Prompt: "How do you manage financial and administrative tasks in your business?"

Benefit: Delegating, sub-contracting, or automating financial and admin tasks can help to save time and allow more focus on other important tasks, leading to increased productivity and efficiency.

Q. Are you managing your time productively? Do you use AI to help you to save time, money & stress? Do you use AI to help you gain clarity, vision, and purpose to embrace, create and live your vision?

1. Yes. All done, planned, documented & automating key tasks.

2. On the case. Working towards it, documenting it.

3. Oops. No, not yet completed (or started).

4. This is all too overwhelming. I Need help with this – fast.

it
stacks
up

SURVIVAL

Marketing Planning

The use of artificial intelligence (AI) in planning marketing endeavours has become increasingly essential in today's fast-paced and data-driven business environment. AI offers a multitude of benefits that can significantly enhance the effectiveness of marketing strategies, from improving customer targeting to streamlining content creation and campaign optimisation.

One of the key advantages of AI in marketing planning is its ability to analyse vast amounts of data quickly and accurately. AI-driven algorithms can sift through customer data, social media interactions, and online behavior to identify patterns and trends that might be missed by human marketers. For instance, AI can recognize when specific demographics engage more with certain types of content, allowing marketers to tailor their messaging accordingly.

AI-powered predictive analytics is another potent tool. It can forecast consumer behavior and help marketers anticipate trends or shifts in the market. For example, an e-commerce platform can use AI to predict which products will be in high demand during specific seasons, enabling them to plan their marketing campaigns and inventory accordingly. Content creation is an area where AI can make a substantial difference. Natural language processing (NLP) algorithms can generate written content, like product descriptions, blog posts, or email copy, quickly and consistently. This not only saves time but also ensures a high level of quality and consistency across various marketing channels.

Personalisation is crucial in modern marketing, and AI excels in this aspect. AI-driven recommendation engines, like those used by streaming platforms, can analyse user preferences and behaviour to suggest products or content that are highly relevant to everyone. This level of personalisation can significantly improve customer engagement and conversion rates.

More importantly, AI can automate certain marketing tasks, such as email marketing, chatbots for customer support, and social media scheduling. This automation not only reduces manual workload but also ensures that marketing efforts are consistent and timely, contributing to the burstiness and effectiveness of campaigns.

In short, the importance of using AI to assist with planning marketing endeavours cannot be overstated. AI can analyse data, predict trends, automate tasks, and personalize content. It can significantly boost marketing performance and efficiency. Embracing AI as a strategic partner in marketing planning is a forward-thinking approach that can lead to a competitive edge in today's highly competitive business landscape.

Each of the points below are split into 4 parts.

- **Challenge:** common issue or obstacle often faced by business owners
- **Fraserism:** a helpful hint, tip, quote, or suggestion to help you in overcoming a challenge.
- **Potential Prompt:** a question, task, and prompt to ask your preferred ai-powered VA.
- **Benefit:** The potential benefit of researching, documenting, executing, automating, and refining a task, process, procedure, or workflow that addresses the underlying challenge.

Challenge: **a lack of thorough market research.**
Fraserism: Conduct in-depth market research to stay informed about current trends and consumer behavior changes.
Potential Prompt: "Can you help us gather the latest data on market trends and consumer behavior?"
Benefit: Researching market trends enables you to make informed decisions and tailor your strategies, accordingly, staying ahead of the curve.

Challenge: **Your marketing strategy lacks flexibility.**
Fraserism: Develop a strategy that includes contingency plans for swift adaptation to unexpected economic shifts.

Potential Prompt: "Can you recommend contingency plans to adjust our marketing strategy when economic shifts occur?"

Benefit: Flexibility in your marketing strategy ensures you can respond effectively to changing economic conditions.

Challenge: **Your marketing plan lacks specificity for the current economic climate.**

Fraserism: Document a marketing plan tailored specifically to the current economic conditions to ensure relevance.

Potential Prompt: "Can your create a detailed marketing plan that addresses the challenges posed by the current economic climate?"

Benefit: A clear and specific plan ensures we are well-prepared to navigate economic uncertainties.

Challenge: **The marketing plan has encountered significant challenges during execution.**

Fraserism: Identify the obstacles and roadblocks hindering plan execution and develop strategies to overcome them.

Potential Prompt: "How can we address the challenges we've encountered while implementing our marketing plan?"

Benefit: Overcoming obstacles ensures that our marketing plan can proceed smoothly.

Challenge A: **Marketing goals and KPIs are not consistently achieved.**

Fraserism: Review and adjust goals and KPIs to be more realistic and achievable within the current economic climate.

Potential Prompt: "How can we reassess our marketing goals and KPIs to improve results?"

Benefit: Realistic goals and KPIs lead to more consistent achievements and a better understanding of success.

Challenge: **Lead generation processes lack automation.**

Fraserism: Explore automation solutions (like itstacksup.com) to streamline lead generation and adapt to market changes.

Potential Prompt: "How can we explore automation options to make lead generation more efficient and responsive?"

Benefit: Automation enhances lead generation efficiency, enabling us to respond quickly to market dynamics.

Challenge: **Marketing content doesn't effectively address audience needs.**

Fraserism: Revise content strategies to focus on understanding and addressing the specific concerns of our target audience.

Potential Prompt: "How can we refine our content strategy to better address the needs of our audience to improve engagement and conversion?"

Benefit: Tailored content resonates more with your audience, improving engagement and conversion.

Challenge: **Lack of AI or machine learning integration for marketing optimisation.**

Fraserism: Explore AI and machine learning applications to analyze and optimise marketing efforts based on real-time data.

Potential Prompt: "How can AI or machine learning tools enhance our marketing strategy for maximum ROI?"

Benefit: AI-driven optimisation leads to more data-driven and effective marketing decisions.

Challenge: **Sales conversion rates have not significantly improved due to marketing efforts.**

Fraserism: Analyse and adjust marketing strategies to focus on improving conversion rates in the current economic climate.

Potential Prompt: "How can we modify our marketing strategies to boost sales conversion rates?"

Benefit: Adjusted strategies can lead to higher conversion rates, translating into increased revenue.

Challenge: **Sales strategy lacks clear documentation and communication.**

Fraserism: Document and communicate the sales strategy clearly to the sales team to ensure alignment and understanding.

Potential Prompt: "Create a clear and concise document outlining our sales strategy and selling process "

Benefit: Clear communication improves team alignment and execution of the sales strategy.

Challenge: **Sales targets are not consistently met.**

Fraserism: Reevaluate sales targets to ensure they are achievable

within the current economic climate.
Potential Prompt: "What are the top 10 best ways to review and adjust our sales targets for best results?"
Benefit: Realistic sales targets enhance motivation and performance within the team.

Challenge: **Bottlenecks and inefficiencies exist in the sales and marketing process.**
Fraserism: Identify and address specific bottlenecks and inefficiencies in the sales process that have emerged due to economic conditions.
Potential Prompt: "How can we pinpoint and resolve bottlenecks in our sales and marketing process?"
Benefit: Eliminating bottlenecks improves sales efficiency, customer experience and ROI.

Challenge: **Routine sales and marketing tasks are not automated.**
Fraserism: Explore automation solutions (like itstackstup.com) to streamline routine sales tasks and adapt to market changes.

Potential Prompt: "How can we implement automation to manage routine sales and marketing tasks to improve efficiency?"
Benefit: Automation reduces manual workload, allowing sales teams to focus on higher-value activities.

Challenge: **Customer support is not adequately prepared for increased enquiries.**
Fraserism: Think of new ways to automate and improve your customer support.
Potential Prompt: "Suggest 12 ways to automate and improve our customer support"
Benefit: Well-prepared customer support ensures timely and satisfactory customer interactions.

Challenge: **Lack of a documented contingency plan that caters for disruptions**
Fraserism: Develop and document a contingency plan to ensure business continuity in the face of potential disruptions.
Potential Prompt: "Suggest a contingency plan to address potential

disruptions that might affect our marketing and sales operations."
Benefit: A contingency plan enhances resilience and preparedness in uncertain situations.

Challenge: **Limited efforts to seek and implement feedback.**
Fraserism: Implement a systematic approach to collect and implement feedback from customers and stakeholders.
Potential Prompt: "Please suggest 12 automated and practical ways to generate feedback from customers and stakeholders."
Benefit: Actively seeking and implementing feedback leads to continuous improvement and customer satisfaction.

Challenge: **Inconsistent monitoring and adjustment of marketing and sales efforts.**
Fraserism: Implement regular monitoring and adjustment processes to respond effectively to changing economic circumstances.
Potential Prompt: "Suggest a potential routine for monitoring and adjusting our marketing and sales efforts in response for maximum results"
Benefit: Consistent monitoring and adjustment lead to more adaptive and effective strategies.

Q. Have you planned, documented, executed, and automated your marketing strategy for the year ahead? Do you use AI to help you to write your marketing strategy? Do you use AI to help you gain clarity, vision, and purpose to achieve your sales and marketing objectives?

1. Yes. All done, planned, documented & in place.
2. On the case. Working towards it, documenting it.
3. Oops. No, not yet completed (or started).
4. This is all too overwhelming. I Need help with this – fast.

153

Lead Generation

Lead generation is the life blood for any business as it is the process of identifying, engaging, and attracting potential customers to use your products, services, or solutions. Without effective lead generation, businesses would struggle to grow and expand their customer base.

Identifying clear routes to market is equally important as it allows businesses to focus their efforts on the most effective channels to reach their target audience. This involves understanding the needs and behaviors of your customers and identifying the channels they are most likely to use when making purchasing decisions.

In terms of perplexity, the process of lead generation and identifying routes to market can be complex and require a certain level of expertise. However, with the right strategies in place, businesses can simplify these processes and increase their chances of success.

The approach to generating leads, enquiries, prospects, appointments, sales, and revenue should be varied and tailored to the needs of each individual customer segment. This can involve using a combination of online and offline channels, such as social media, email marketing, events, and networking, to reach potential customers and build relationships with them.

Just remember, if you want to maximize signups, registrations, appointments, and sales then one of the first steps you should take is in creating a customer avatar to clearly outline who is an ideal customer and where do they congregate online. (We share one on our website at itstacksup.com.) Identifying clear routes to market online, offline and via mobile devices is critical for the success of any business. By using a combination of strategies tailored to the needs of their customers, businesses can increase their chances of attracting, engaging, and converting leads into sales.

Each of the points below are split into 4 parts.

- **Challenge:** common issue or obstacle often faced by business owners
- **Fraserism:** a helpful hint, tip, quote, or suggestion to help you in overcoming a challenge.
- **Potential Prompt:** a question, task, and prompt to ask your preferred ai-powered VA.
- **Benefit:** The potential benefit of researching, documenting, executing, automating, and refining a task, process, procedure, or workflow that addresses the underlying challenge.

Challenge: **understanding the needs and wants of your target audience without an avatar**
Fraserism: Creating a customer avatar helps to gain a deeper understanding of your target audience's needs, wants, and pain points, which in turn helps in creating targeted marketing campaigns that appeal to their interests.
Potential Prompt: How can I create a customer avatar to better understand my target audience?
Benefit: Creating a customer avatar helps to tailor marketing campaigns, resulting in higher engagement rates and a greater chance of converting leads into customers.

Challenge: **Limited reach in target markets due to lack of JVs or channel partners**
Fraserism: Partnering with channel partners or JV partners helps to expand your reach in target markets by leveraging their existing networks.
Potential Prompt: How can I find the right channel partners or JV partners to expand my reach in target markets?
Benefit: Partnering with channel partners or JV partners helps to expand your reach in target markets, resulting in increased brand awareness and potential leads.

Challenge: **reaching and engaging with potential customers in different geographic locations.**

Fraserism: Using a sales team, distributors or agents helps to reach and engage with potential customers in different geographic locations by leveraging their local knowledge and expertise.

Potential Prompt: How can I leverage sales teams, distributors, or agents to reach potential customers in different geographic locations?

Benefit: Using a sales team, distributors or agents helps to expand your reach and engage with potential customers in different geographic locations, resulting in increased leads and potential sales.

Challenge: **Inability to engage with target audience in real-time.**

Fraserism: Using Live video streaming helps to engage with your target audience in real-time, providing opportunities for Q&A sessions and building trust.

Potential Prompt: How can I use Live video streaming to engage with my target audience?

Benefit: Using Live video streaming helps to build trust and engagement with your target audience, resulting in increased leads and potential sales.

Challenge: **Difficulty in generating leads through innovative online marketing methods.**

Fraserism: Using webinars or video marketing helps to generate leads by providing valuable information and building trust with your target audience.

Potential Prompt: How can I use webinars or video marketing to generate leads?

Benefit: Using webinars or video marketing helps to build trust and generate leads by providing valuable information to your target audience.

Challenge: **Limited reach and engagement on social media platforms.**

Fraserism: Using social networking or business networking helps to expand your reach and engage with potential customers by leveraging social media platforms.

Potential Prompt: How can I use social networking or business networking to expand my reach and engage with potential customers?

Benefit: Using social networking or business networking helps to

156

expand your reach and engage with potential customers, resulting in increased brand awareness and potential leads.

Challenge: **Difficulty in engaging with potential customers through telemarketing.**
Fraserism: Using telemarketing or telecanvassing helps to engage with potential customers through phone calls, providing opportunities to build trust and answer questions.
Potential Prompt: How can I use telemarketing or telecanvassing to engage with potential customers?
Benefit: Using telemarketing or telecanvassing helps to engage with potential customers through phone calls, resulting in increased leads and potential sales.

Challenge: **Difficulty in organizing and conducting meetings with potential customers in different geographic locations.**
Fraserism: Using teleconferences helps to organize and conduct meetings with potential customers in different geographic locations, providing opportunities to build relationships and answer questions.
Potential Prompt: How can I use live streaming or webinars to organize and conduct meetings with potential customers in different geographic locations?
Benefit: Using live streaming helps to organize and conduct meetings with potential customers in different geographic locations, resulting in increased leads and potential sales.

Challenge: **Lack of social proof can hinder trust and credibility with potential customers.**
Fraserism: Encourage satisfied customers to provide feedback and testimonials, and prominently display them on your website and social media channels. Consider offering incentives for customers who provide feedback or referrals.
Potential Prompt: "How can I increase social proof for my business?"
Benefit: Building social proof can help establish trust and credibility with potential customers, which can increase the likelihood of generating leads and conversions.

Challenge: **Limited local reach and visibility in your immediate area.**

Fraserism: Utilize leaflet distribution or local newspaper classified ads to reach a local audience. Offer special promotions or discounts to incentivize new customers to engage with your business.

Potential Prompt: "How can I increase local reach for my business?"

Benefit: By targeting a local audience, you may be able to generate more leads and conversions from customers in your immediate area.

Challenge: **Limited customer referrals can hinder lead generation efforts.**

Fraserism: Implement a referral marketing system to encourage existing customers to refer new customers. Offer incentives such as discounts or free products/services for successful referrals.

Potential Prompt: "How can I increase customer referrals for my business?"

Benefit: Referral marketing can be an effective way to generate new leads and customers through the word-of-mouth of satisfied customers. (We also share a referral marketing system that works online and offline and takes 10 seconds to deploy – available in the Skillutions area of our site.)

Challenge: **Lack of audio content**

Fraserism: Publish audio books or podcasts to reach potential customers who prefer audio formats. Utilize platforms such as iTunes to distribute audio content to a wider audience.

Potential Prompt: "How can I reach customers who prefer audio formats?"

Benefit: By offering audio content, you can reach potential customers who may not engage with other formats and increase the likelihood of generating leads and conversions.

Challenge: **Ineffective SEO or PPC strategy may limit visibility to potential customers.**

Fraserism: Develop and implement a targeted SEO or PPC strategy to improve visibility to potential customers. Consider working with a digital marketing agency or consultant to develop an effective strategy.

Potential Prompt: "How can I improve my seo and ppc marketing strategy?"

Benefit: An effective digital marketing strategy can increase visibility to potential customers, which can lead to increased leads and conversions.

Challenge: **Limited exposure as a speaker or blogger**
Fraserism: Position yourself as a keynote speaker or guest speaker at industry events, or as a blogger or guest blogger on relevant websites. This can increase exposure to potential customers and establish expertise in your field and I have now presented on 4 continents around the globe.
Potential Prompt: "How can I increase my visibility as an industry expert?"
Benefit: Establishing yourself as an industry expert can increase credibility and trust with potential customers, which can lead to increased leads and conversions.

Challenge: **Ineffective offline advertising strategy may limit visibility to potential customers.**
Fraserism: Develop and implement a targeted advertising strategy, both online and offline. Utilize classified or display advertising as appropriate to reach potential customers.
Potential Prompt: "How can I improve my advertising strategy offline?"
Benefit: An effective advertising strategy can increase visibility to potential customers, which can lead to increased leads and conversions.

Challenge: **Limited reach to potential customers who use mobile devices.**
Fraserism: Share relevant APPS, widgets, or extensions in Google Play Store to reach potential customers who use mobile devices. Consider working with a mobile app development agency to develop relevant apps or widgets.
Potential Prompt: "How can I reach potential customers who use mobile devices?"
Benefit: Reaching potential customers who use mobile devices can increase the likelihood of generating leads and conversions from this demographic.

Q. Are you generating enough leads for your products, services, and solutions? Do you use AI to help you to generate traffic, signups & registrations? Do you use AI to help you gain clarity, vision, and purpose to embrace, create and live your vision?

1. Yes. All done, planned, documented & implanted to generate leads.
2. On the case. Working towards it, documenting it.
3. Oops. No, not yet completed (or started).
4. This is all too overwhelming. I Need help with this – fast.

Social Media Marketing

Social media marketing is an essential component of launching, running, and scaling a business in the digital age. Social media platforms provide businesses with the opportunity to connect with their target audience, increase brand awareness, and drive traffic to their website. Some of the most popular social media platforms for marketing include Facebook, Instagram, Twitter, LinkedIn, and TikTok.

Facebook is an excellent platform for businesses of all sizes, with a user base of over 2 billion people. The platform offers a range of advertising options, including sponsored posts, carousel ads, and video ads, which can be targeted based on demographics, interests, and behaviors. Instagram is a highly visual platform that is ideal for businesses in the fashion, beauty, and lifestyle industries. The platform also offers advertising options such as sponsored posts and Stories ads.

Twitter is a platform that allows businesses to connect with their audience through real-time conversations. The platform is ideal for businesses that want to engage with their customers and respond to their queries quickly. LinkedIn is a professional networking platform that is ideal for B2B businesses. The platform allows businesses to connect with other professionals in their industry and promote their products and services.

TikTok has exploded in growth gaining popularity, particularly among younger audiences with many uploaded videos generating millions of views. The platform is highly visual and is ideal for businesses in the entertainment and fashion industries. Businesses can use TikTok to create short, engaging videos that showcase their products or services.

To effectively manage a social media marketing campaign, businesses need to have a unified martech stack. A martech stack is a collection of tools and technologies that businesses use to attract, engage, and convert customers. It can include tools for social media management, email marketing, CRM, analytics, and more.

One example of a unified martech stack is ItStacksUp.com, which offers a range of tools and services that can help businesses streamline their customer journey and maximize engagement. The platform offers tools for social media management, email marketing, and analytics, all in one place. This can help businesses save time and resources by managing their marketing campaigns more efficiently.

Q. What IP could you license or franchise on a per country basis? ☐

Each of the points below are split into 4 parts.

- **Challenge:** common issue or obstacle often faced by business owners
- **Fraserism:** a helpful hint, tip, quote, or suggestion to help you in overcoming a challenge.
- **Potential Prompt:** a question, task, and prompt to ask your preferred ai-powered VA.
- **Benefit:** The potential benefit of researching, documenting, executing, automating, and refining a task, process, procedure, or workflow that addresses the underlying challenge.

Challenge: **Wanting an increase in website traffic**
Fraserism: Consider analyzing your current social media content to identify areas for improvement. Ensure that your posts are relevant, engaging, and shareable. Experiment with different types of content, such as videos or infographics, to attract more attention from social media users.
Potential Prompt: What steps can I take to improve the engagement and shareability of my social media content?
Benefit: By improving the quality and relevance of your social media content, you can attract more attention from social media users and increase the likelihood of them visiting your website.

Challenge: **Your social media posts not receiving as much engagement**

Fraserism: Consider experimenting with different types of content, such as live videos or interactive polls, to increase engagement with your social media followers. Additionally, engage with your followers by responding to comments and asking for their opinions or feedback on your content.

Potential Prompt: How can I increase my engagement with my social media followers?

Benefit: By increasing engagement with your social media followers, you can build relationships and increase the likelihood of them visiting your website and landing pages.

Challenge: **Your social media ads not resulting in conversions or sales**

Fraserism: Consider refining your target audience and adjusting your ad messaging to better appeal to their needs and interests. Additionally, ensure that your landing pages are optimized for conversions and that the user experience is seamless.

Potential Prompt: What steps can I take to improve the conversion rate of my social media ads?

Benefit: By improving the conversion rate of your social media ads, you can increase the return on investment and drive more revenue for your business.

Challenge: **Wanting more referred traffic to your website**

Fraserism: Consider identifying relevant influencers in your industry and reaching out to them to establish a partnership or sponsorship. Alternatively, consider creating your own influencer program to attract relevant influencers to promote your brand.

Potential Prompt: How can I leverage influencer marketing to drive traffic to my website?

Benefit: By partnering with influencers, you can increase the reach of your brand and drive more traffic to your website through their followers and fans.

Challenge: **Not utilizing user-generated content**

Fraserism: Consider encouraging your followers and customers to share their experiences with your brand on social media and feature their content on your own channels. This can increase engagement and credibility with your audience.

Potential Prompt: How can I use user-generated content to promote my website and landing pages?

Benefit: By featuring user-generated content, you can increase engagement and authenticity with your audience, and drive more traffic to your website and landing pages.

Challenge: **Not using paid social media ads to target specific audiences**

Fraserism: Consider investing in paid social media ads to reach a larger and more targeted audience. Use audience targeting and ad optimization to ensure that your ads are being seen by the right people.

Potential Prompt: How can I use paid social media ads to drive traffic to my website?

Benefit: By using paid social media ads, you can reach a larger and more targeted audience, and increase the likelihood of driving more traffic to your website and landing pages.

Challenge: **Having trouble measuring the success of your social media marketing**

Fraserism: One way to measure the success of your social media marketing efforts is to use Google Analytics to track the traffic coming from your social media channels to your website. Set up specific goals and conversion tracking to measure the number of leads generated from social media. Use UTM codes to track the effectiveness of individual social media posts and campaigns.

Potential Prompt: How can I measure the effectiveness of my social media marketing efforts in terms of website traffic and lead generation?

Benefit: By tracking the success of your social media marketing efforts, you can identify what works and what doesn't, and adjust your strategy accordingly to improve your results.

Challenge: **Not using targeted social media ads to reach potential customers**

Fraserism: Utilize the targeting options available on social media platforms to reach potential customers who are most likely to be interested in your products or services. Create audience personas based on demographics, interests, and behaviors, and tailor your ads to their needs and preferences.

Potential Prompt: How can I use social media ads to target potential customers based on their demographics and interests?

Benefit: By targeting your social media ads to specific audiences, you can increase the effectiveness of your marketing efforts and improve your return on investment.

Challenge: **Struggling to keep social media content fresh and engaging**

Fraserism: Use a mix of different types of content, such as blog posts, images, videos, infographics, and interactive content. Experiment with different formats and styles to see what resonates with your audience. Ask for feedback and engage with your followers to build a sense of community and encourage user-generated content.

Potential Prompt: What can I do to keep my social media content fresh and engaging for my followers?

Benefit: By creating engaging social media content, you can increase the visibility of your brand and drive more traffic to your website.

Challenge: **Not collaborating with other businesses or influencers on social media**

Fraserism: Identify potential collaborators who share your target audience and brand values. Reach out to them to propose a collaboration or partnership that will benefit both parties. Share each other's content, run joint promotions, or co-create content that will resonate with your shared audience.

Potential Prompt: How can I collaborate with other businesses or influencers on social media to expand my reach and drive traffic to my website?

Benefit: By collaborating with other businesses or influencers, you can reach new audiences and gain credibility and authority in your industry.

 Q. Are you considering franchising or licensing your intellectual property? Do you use AI to help you to

better manage your franchise opportunity? Do you use AI to help you gain clarity, vision, and purpose to embrace, create and live your vision?

1. Yes. All done, planned, documented & implemented in the business.

2. On the case. Working towards it, documenting it.

3. Oops. No, not yet completed (or started).

4. This is all too overwhelming. I Need help with this – fast.

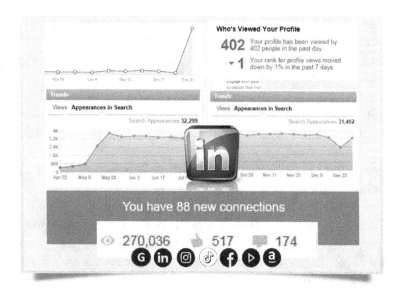

Sales copywriting

When it comes to marketing your business, having a persuasive, engaging, and compelling sales copy is crucial. This type of copy is designed to grab the reader's attention and convince them to act, whether it's making a purchase, signing up for a service, or filling out a form. But to create effective sales copy, you may need to consider using a copywriting system such as: -

The 4 C's: Capture, Connect, Convince, Close
The 4 C's system is a copywriting approach that involves capturing the reader's attention, connecting with them by addressing their needs or pain points, convincing them that your product or service is the solution they need, and closing the sale with a strong call to action.

Story, Understanding, Credibility, Context, Emotion, Solution, and Seal the Deal
The S.U.C.C.E.S.S. Framework is a copywriting approach that involves telling a story that resonates with the reader, demonstrating understanding of their pain points, establishing credibility, providing context for the solution you offer, connecting emotionally, presenting your solution, and sealing the deal with a compelling call to action.

The C.A.R.E. System: Connect, Address, Resolve, Explain
The C.A.R.E. System is a copywriting approach that involves connecting with the reader on a personal level, addressing their specific pain points or objections, resolving those pain points with your solution, and explaining how your solution can make their life better.

The P.A.C.T. Formula: Promise, Action, Confidence, Trust
The P.A.C.T. Formula is a copywriting system that involves making a promise to the reader, encouraging them to take action, building confidence in your solution, and establishing trust with the reader.

The R.E.S.T. Method: Research, Engage, Solve, Test
The R.E.S.T. Method is a copywriting approach that involves conducting thorough research on your target audience and their pain

points, engaging with them through your copy, solving their problems with your solution, and testing and optimizing your copy for maximum effectiveness.

You want your sales copy to be easy to read and understand, so that your message comes across clearly. If your copy is too complex, it can be difficult for readers to follow along, and they may lose interest. On the other hand, if your copy is too simple, it may not hold their attention. Finding the right balance is key.

We humans tend to write using longer complex sentences alongside shorter ones. This can make your writing more interesting and engaging to read. However, be aware that AI-generated sentences tend to be more uniform, lacking this variation and can be quite short, un-interesting and lacking emotion. Remember in sales and marketing, people buy with their emotions, and justify their buying decisions using logic and reason. You want your key marketing message to stir the emotions of your target audience and encourage them to take action.

To create good engaging sales copy, and have a killer marketing message, your copy should be impactful, easy to understand, but also engaging and varied enough to hold the reader's attention.

Just like the sun newspaper headline that sold thousands of copies of newspapers. This was achieved through careful editing, revising, and optimising, and using persuasive language and an attention-grabbing headline. In my opinion, it was genius and highlighted a surprising result of a game of football between a small Scottish highland's team "Caledonian Thistle" and premier league team giant – "Celtic."

So, writing a persuasive, engaging, and compelling sales copy is essential to enhance your marketing message and grow your business. By optimizing your copy to follow certain copywriting formulas and having a good CTA (call to action), you can create copy that is both easy to read and interesting, help you to stand out from the competition and capture the attention of your target audience and to instill them to action to by clicking on a button or visit your site.

Q. How would you write your elevator pitch without mentioning service, quality, reliability, or price? ☐

Each of the points below are split into 4 parts.

- **Challenge:** common issue or obstacle often faced by business owners
- **Fraserism:** a helpful hint, tip, quote, or suggestion to help you in overcoming a challenge.
- **Potential Prompt:** a question, task, and prompt to ask your preferred ai-powered VA.
- **Benefit:** The potential benefit of researching, documenting, executing, automating, and refining a task, process, procedure, or workflow that addresses the underlying challenge.

Challenge: **No marketing communications strategy document**
Fraserism: If you don't have a written marketing communications strategy document, it's important to create one. Start by setting clear objectives, identifying your target audience, and understanding their pain points and motivations. Develop a clear message and identify the channels you will use to reach your audience.
Potential Prompt: What steps can I take to create a written marketing communications strategy document?
Benefit: A written marketing communications strategy document will help you stay focused on your objectives and ensure that all your marketing activities are aligned with your goals.

Challenge: **No portfolio of offline marketing collateral**
Fraserism: If you don't have a portfolio of offline marketing collateral, it's important to create one. This can include brochures, flyers, business cards, and other printed materials. Consider collaborating with a graphic designer to ensure that your materials are visually appealing and consistent with your brand.
Potential Prompt: How can I create a portfolio of offline marketing collateral?
Benefit: Having a portfolio of offline marketing collateral can help you reach potential customers who may not be online or who prefer physical materials.

Challenge: **Writing all your own sales & marketing "copy"**
Fraserism: If you don't write all your own sales and marketing copy, it's important to collaborate with a skilled copywriter who can help you craft compelling and persuasive messages. A copywriter can help you identify your unique selling proposition and create messaging that resonates with your target audience.
Potential Prompt: Can you write an advert, and letter to sell [bathtubs]?
Benefit: Collaborating with a skilled copywriter can help you create more effective marketing messages that drive conversions and revenue.

Challenge: **No "lead magnet," digital asset or "value BONUS"?**
Fraserism: If you don't have a portfolio of lead magnets, digital assets, or value bonuses, it's important to create them using tools like canva.com. Lead magnets can include free e-books, whitepapers, webinars, and other valuable resources that your target audience will find useful.
Potential Prompt: What types of lead magnets or digital assets should I create for my business?
Benefit: Offering valuable lead magnets or digital assets can help you build trust with potential customers and encourage them to take the next step in the buying process.

Challenge: **Not planning, produce, present, and promote your own webinars**
Fraserism: If you run your own webinars, it's important to start.

Webinars can be an effective way to educate your audience, build trust, and generate leads. Start by identifying a topic that will be of interest to your target audience and develop a clear plan for your webinar.

Potential Prompt: What tools and software do I need to plan, produce, present, and promote a webinar?

Benefit: Hosting webinars can help you build your brand, generate leads, and establish yourself as a thought leader in your industry.

Challenge: **Do you present and promote your own videos?**

Fraserism: If you don't produce, present, and promote your own videos, then I urge you to start. Videos that are engaging, shocking or funny can often go viral and achieve millions of views and comments whilst educating your audience, building trust, and generating leads. Start by identifying a topic that will be of interest to your target audience, and develop publicity for your products, services, and solutions.

Potential Prompt: How can I improve the promotion of my videos?

Benefit: Hosting videos on youtube.com can help you build your brand, generate leads, and establish yourself as a thought leader in your industry, sector, or niche.

Potential Prompt: What are some strategies to ensure regular social media posting across multiple platforms?

Benefit: By scheduling social media posts in advance, you can save time and ensure a consistent presence on social media, which can help increase engagement and brand awareness.

Challenge: **Not having a collection of CTAs (calls to action)**

Fraserism: Create a list of effective CTAs that can be used across various marketing channels, such as email, website, social media, and ads. Make sure they are clear and compelling, and test different variations to see what works best for your audience.

Potential Prompt: Can you provide some examples of effective calls to action that can be used in marketing campaigns?

Benefit: By having a collection of effective CTAs, you can save time and improve the effectiveness of your marketing efforts, leading to increased conversions and sales.

Challenge: **Not upselling website visitors and customers with OTOs**

Fraserism: Implement a system for presenting relevant upsell offers to customers, such as a pop-up or a redirection to a dedicated page. Make sure the offer is compelling and adds value to the customer's purchase.

Potential Prompt: How can I effectively upsell customers with one time offers without being too pushy?

Benefit: By offering relevant upsell offers, you can increase the average order value and generate more revenue from each customer.

Challenge: **Not having a collection of headlines to test and use for blogs, ads, articles etc.**

Fraserism: Create a swipe file of effective headlines from various sources, such as magazines, websites, and competitor ads. Use this as inspiration to create your own attention-grabbing headlines, and test different variations to see what works best for your audience.

Potential Prompt: What are some tips for creating attention-grabbing headlines for my blog posts?

Benefit: By using effective headlines, you can increase the likelihood of readers engaging with your content and taking action.

Challenge: **Not having a collection of classified ads to test and use for online & offline**

Fraserism: Create a collection of effective classified ads for various sources, such as newspapers, trade magazines and social networking platforms. Use canva.com to create your own ads, and test different variations to see what works best for your target audience and distribution channels.

Potential Prompt: How can I create effective classified ads for my business?

Benefit: By using effective classified ads, you can generate leads and drive traffic to your website or physical location.

Challenge: **Not having a collection of images/photos to test and use for sharing online?**

Fraserism: Create a library of high-quality images using pixabay, midjourney or nightcafe that are relevant and unique to your brand and target audience. Use these in social media posts, ads, and website content to make your marketing materials more visually appealing and engaging.

Potential Prompt: What are some best practices for using images in social media marketing?

Benefit: By using high-quality images, you can increase engagement and improve the overall effectiveness of your marketing efforts.

Challenge: **Not having a nurture sequence?**

Fraserism: Create a series or sequence of automated emails to be sent to someone who has signed up for your lead magnet, A powerful wee tip: Set the send interval to 1, 2, 5,7 14, 21 and 28 days apart so as not to overwhelm sending several emails in one day and ensure you personalize the emails with tags.

Potential Prompt: Please create a series of 5 emails to be sent to enquire about our [coaching services]?

Benefit: Having a personalized automated nurture sequence can help you to increase conversions, reduce churn, improve customer loyalty, and extend the lifetime value of customers.

Q. Are you using AI to write your promotional sales copy? Do you use AI to help you to save time, money & stress? Do you use AI to help you gain clarity, vision, and purpose to embrace, create and live your vision?

1. Yes. All done, planned, documented & written by AI.

2. On the case. Working towards it, documenting it.

3. Oops. No, not yet completed (or started).

4. This is all too overwhelming. I Need help with this – fast.

Sales Prospecting

LinkedIn is a powerful social media platform that allows businesses to connect with potential customers and build relationships. It offers a range of features, including company pages, groups, and messaging, which can help businesses find and engage with prospective customers. Sales professionals can use LinkedIn to research prospects, join relevant groups, and participate in discussions to establish themselves as thought leaders in their industry. More importantly, if you have completed your customer avatar it's going to make finding, targeting and engaging suspects and potential customers with a compelling sales message – much easier.

Phone calls are a direct and personal way to reach out to prospects. They allow sales professionals to communicate the value of their products or services and address any questions or concerns that prospects may have. Whilst many sales organisations have automated this process and use "power dialers," personalisation is key when making sales calls, and it is important to tailor the conversation to the prospect's needs and interests.

Ensure you have crafted your elevator pitch or "30 second commercial "to make a highly impactful and engaging direct message, letter, email, or phone call.

Direct mail is a traditional marketing method that can still be effective in today's digital age. Sending a well-crafted direct mail piece can help businesses stand out from the competition and make an impression on prospects. Direct mail can also be personalized with the prospect's name, company, and other relevant details to increase its impact.

Email is a cost-effective way to reach many prospects quickly and easily. However, it is important to ensure that the email is personalized, relevant, and provides value to the prospect. Sales professionals should also follow up on their emails to increase the chances of a response.

Other tools such as skype, messenger, chatbots and WhatsApp are often used to reach out and start engaging with others, and many of these tools can also been automated and connected to a CRM system or autoresponder.

So, sales prospecting and direct outreach are crucial activities for any business looking to grow its customer base and increase revenue. I cover direct outreach on LinkedIn in my book "Pipeline" and have a complete system to help you do this inside itstacksup.com. LinkedIn, phone, direct mail, and email are all effective channels for reaching out to generate leads, however, I'd recommended businesses should use a combination of these methods to maximize their results.

Q. How many leads do you need to generate the revenue you want? ☐

Each of the points below are split into 4 parts.
- **Challenge:** common issue or obstacle often faced by business owners
- **Fraserism:** a helpful hint, tip, quote, or suggestion to help you in overcoming a challenge.
- **Potential Prompt:** a question, task, and prompt to ask your preferred ai-powered VA.
- **Benefit:** The potential benefit of researching, documenting, executing, automating, and refining a task, process, procedure, or workflow that addresses the underlying challenge.

Challenge: **Not having a completed customer avatar**
Fraserism: As previously mentioned, develop a detailed customer avatar that includes demographics, interests, pain points, and goals. Use this avatar as a guide for all sales prospecting and outreach efforts on LinkedIn by DM, by phone and email.
Potential Prompt: What specific pain points and goals do your ideal customers have, and how can you tailor your outreach to address these needs?
Benefit: A completed customer avatar can help businesses target the right audience and increase the effectiveness of their sales efforts.

Challenge: **Not knowing where potential customers congregate online**

Fraserism: Conduct market research to identify online platforms where potential customers are active. Use this information to focus sales prospecting and outreach efforts on these platforms.

Potential Prompt: Where do your ideal customers spend their time online, and how can you reach them effectively on these platforms?

Benefit: Knowing where potential customers congregate online can help businesses maximize the reach and impact of their sales efforts.

Challenge: **Not having a defined sales process**

Fraserism: Map out a clear and defined sales process that outlines each step from prospecting to closing the sale. Use this process as a guide for all sales outreach and follow-up efforts.

Potential Prompt: What are the specific steps in your current sales process, and how can you streamline and optimize each step for maximum efficiency?

Benefit: Having a defined sales process can help businesses stay organized and focused, leading to more efficient and effective sales outreach.

Challenge: **Not segmenting your market and using better targeting**

Fraserism: Divide the market into smaller segments based on demographics, interests, and needs. Use these segments to target prospects more effectively and tailor outreach efforts to their specific needs.

Potential Prompt: How can you segment your market effectively to better target prospective clients, and what specific outreach strategies can you use for each segment?

Benefit: Segmenting the market can help businesses target prospects more effectively and increase the impact of their sales outreach.

Challenge: **Not visiting other members' profiles on LinkedIn or following up visitors to yours**

Fraserism: Regularly visit the profiles of potential customers and engage with them through comments or direct messages. Follow up with visitors to your own profile to build relationships and stay top of mind.

Potential Prompt: How can you engage with potential customers on LinkedIn and follow up with visitors to your own profile to build relationships and establish credibility?

Benefit: Engaging with potential customers on LinkedIn and following up with visitors to your own profile can help build relationships and increase the effectiveness of sales outreach.

Challenge: **Not using LinkedIn Sales Navigator or a prospecting system like "Pipeline."**

Fraserism: Use LinkedIn Navigator or a pipeline system such as itstacksup.com to organize and track sales prospects and outreach efforts. This can help businesses stay organized and focused, leading to more efficient and effective outreach.

Potential Prompt: How can you use LinkedIn Navigator or a pipeline system to organize and track your sales prospects and outreach efforts, and how can this help improve your sales results?

Benefit: Using LinkedIn Navigator or a pipeline system can help businesses stay organized and focused, leading to more efficient and effective sales outreach.

Challenge: **Not knowing how many leads are needed to achieve revenue goals**

Fraserism: Determine how many leads are needed to achieve revenue goals and set specific targets for lead generation and outreach efforts. More importantly, in estimating the time needed and conversions required to generate ROI from your efforts.

Potential Prompt: How many leads do you need to achieve your revenue goals, and what specific strategies can you use to generate these leads?

Challenge: **Finding quality leads can be time-consuming and difficult to manage manually.**

Fraserism: Consider using lead generation software or service that automates the process of finding and nurturing leads.

Potential Prompt: "How do you currently generate leads for your business?"

Benefit: An automated prospecting system can save time and increase efficiency by identifying and nurturing leads, resulting in a higher conversion rate.

Challenge: **Closing sales can be a long and difficult process**
Fraserism: Implement a sales management system to help automate and streamline the sales process.
Potential Prompt: "Can you walk me through your current sales process?"
Benefit: An automated sales process can help increase productivity, reduce costs, and improve the customer experience, resulting in increased revenue.

Challenge: **Follow-up is essential for closing sales, but can be time-consuming**
Fraserism: Implement a customer relationship management (CRM) system to automate follow-up tasks and improve customer communication.
Potential Prompt: "How do you currently follow-up with leads and customers?"
Benefit: An automated follow-up system can help increase customer retention, improve customer satisfaction, and increase sales conversions.

Challenge: **Understanding what prospective clients value and are willing to pay for**
Fraserism: Conduct market research to understand the needs and desires of your target audience and develop solutions that meet those needs.
Potential Prompt: "What do you think your target audience values most in your product/service?"
Benefit: Knowing what your prospective clients value can help you tailor your offerings to meet their needs and increase sales.

Challenge: **Understanding what prospective clients don't want**
Fraserism: Conduct market research and collect feedback from current and prospective clients to identify pain points and areas for improvement.
Potential Prompt: "What are some common complaints or concerns you hear from your target audience?"
Benefit: Understanding what your prospective clients don't want can help you avoid mistakes and make improvements that will increase customer satisfaction and retention.

Challenge: **Prospective clients may have questions or concerns that can make or break a sale.**

Fraserism: Anticipate common questions or concerns and prepare answers ahead of time.

Potential Prompt: "What are some common questions or concerns you hear from your target audience in the [construction industry] looking for [plan hire]"

Benefit: Anticipating and addressing common questions and concerns can help build trust with prospective clients and increase sales conversions.

Challenge: **Standing out from competitors can be difficult**

Fraserism: Develop a unique value proposition and clearly communicate it to prospective clients in your LinkedIn profile and headline. For inspiration, feel free to visit my profile on LinkedIn at: https://www.linkedin.com/in/martech-keynote-speaker-coach/

Potential Prompt: "What do you think sets your business apart from competitors in your industry?"

Benefit: Knowing and communicating your unique value proposition can help differentiate your business and increase sales.

Challenge: **Understanding potential barriers to sales**

Fraserism: Collect feedback from current and prospective clients to identify common objections or concerns.

Potential Prompt: "What are some common reasons why prospective clients choose not to work with you?"

Benefit: Understanding potential barriers to sales can help you make improvements that will increase customer satisfaction

Q. Are you performing direct outreach? Do you use AI to help you to save time, money & stress? Do you use AI to help you gain clarity, vision, and purpose to embrace, create and live your vision?

1. Yes. All done, planned, documented & executed by AI.

2. On the case. Working towards it, documenting it.

3. Oops. No, not yet completed (or started).

4. This is all too overwhelming. I Need help with this – fast.

Sales & Marketing Funnel

Developing and automating a sales and marketing funnel is a critical step for businesses seeking to simplify their customer journey and uncover new sales possibilities. With the help of a customized martech platform, companies can automate workflows and processes, effectively nurturing leads and guiding them through the sales funnel with minimal effort.

Consider the advantages of having the ability to create landing pages without incurring the cost of hiring a web designer, or automating your workflows, scoring leads, safeguarding, and protecting customer data, and creating more sales opportunities using accessible tools, all while increasing the likelihood of closing more sales with an automated follow-up nurture sequence. The time, money, and stress savings alone can be enormous.

Having your own martech platform saves time and resources while ensuring that every lead is properly tracked and engaged with at every stage of the sales funnel. A well-designed sales and marketing funnel utilizing a martech platform also allows businesses to segment their audience and target them with customized content and messaging, increasing the likelihood of converting them into paying customers and building long-term loyalty.

Automating the sales and marketing funnel also yields valuable data and insights into customer behavior, allowing businesses to refine their approach and improve their overall marketing strategy. This information can be used to pinpoint areas of the funnel that require optimization and enhance the entire customer journey for better results.

Creating and automating a sales and marketing funnel is a critical step for any business that wants to simplify its customer journey, enhance its marketing strategy, and unlock new sales opportunities. It helps businesses save time and resources, while also offering valuable data and insights that can be utilized to continually improve the sales process.

Q. How many different software solutions do you use to automate all your marketing? ☐

Each of the points below are split into 4 parts.

- **Challenge:** common issue or obstacle often faced by business owners
- **Fraserism:** a helpful hint, tip, quote, or suggestion to help you in overcoming a challenge.
- **Potential Prompt:** a question, task, and prompt to ask your preferred ai-powered VA.
- **Benefit:** The potential benefit of researching, documenting, executing, automating, and refining a task, process, procedure, or workflow that addresses the underlying challenge.

Challenge: **No clearly defined sales and marketing process and funnel**
Fraserism: Develop a clear sales and marketing process and funnel that outlines the steps from lead generation to closing the sale. Use CRM to track customer interactions and automate parts of the process.
Potential Prompt: "What steps do you recommend for creating a sales and marketing process that is easy to track and optimize?"
Benefit: With a defined sales and marketing process, you can better track and measure the effectiveness of your efforts, identify areas for improvement, and make data-driven decisions to improve your ROI.

Challenge: **a fragmented and disjointed online marketing funnel, and sales process**
Fraserism: Integrate your martech stack and sales process into your website to create a seamless experience for prospects and customers. Use tools like Zapier or API connections to streamline workflows and automate processes.
Potential Prompt: "How can I integrate my martech stack and sales process into my website to create a more cohesive experience?"
Benefit: By integrating your martech stack and sales process into your website, you can provide a seamless experience for prospects

and customers, which can improve conversions, sales, and customer satisfaction.

Challenge: **No privacy center or GDPR compliance**
Fraserism: Create a privacy center on your website that outlines your privacy policy, how you collect and use customer data, and how customers can control their data. Ensure that your martech stack is GDPR-compliant and that you have processes in place to manage data requests and breaches.
Potential Prompt: "What are the steps I need to take to ensure my website and martech stack are GDPR-compliant and have a privacy center?"
Benefit: By being GDPR-compliant and having a privacy center, you can build trust with your customers and protect your business from legal and reputational consequences.

Challenge: **No clearly defined sales message for each step in your marketing funnel,**
Fraserism: Develop a clear and consistent sales message for each step in your marketing funnel that communicates the unique value proposition of your product or service. Use customer data and feedback to refine your message over time.
Potential Prompt: "How can I create a clear and consistent sales message for each step in my marketing funnel?"
Benefit: With a clear and consistent sales message, you can communicate value and differentiate yourself from competitors, which can improve conversions and sales.

Challenge: **No automated solution for each step of your marketing funnel**
Fraserism: Use marketing automation tools to automate repetitive tasks and processes throughout your marketing funnel, from lead generation to lead nurturing to closing the sale.
Potential Prompt: "What are some ways I can automate my marketing funnel to engage with prospects and customers more effectively?"
Benefit: By automating parts of your marketing funnel, you can save time, reduce costs, and improve the overall efficiency and effectiveness of your sales and marketing efforts.

Challenge: **No automated process for following ups or automated nurture sequence**

Fraserism: Use an automated CRM or sales tool to follow up with prospects and customers, track interactions and behavior, and send personalized messages and offers based on their needs and interests.

Potential Prompt: "What are some ways I can use automation to improve my follow-up and sales process?"

Benefit: By automating parts of your sales process, you can improve efficiency, reduce errors, and increase revenue by upselling and cross-selling to existing customers.

Challenge: **No lead scoring system or pipeline management system**

Fraserism: Implement a lead scoring system that assigns points to leads based on their level of engagement with your brand and their behavior on your website. This can help your sales team focus on the most promising leads and increase conversions.

Potential Prompt: "What criteria do you currently use to prioritize leads, and how do you ensure that your sales team is focusing on the most promising opportunities?"

Benefit: A lead scoring system can help improve the efficiency and effectiveness of your sales team by allowing them to prioritize their efforts and focus on the most promising leads.

Challenge: **No clear content strategy, calendar**

Fraserism: Develop a content strategy and calendar that outlines your goals, target audience, content topics, and publishing schedule. This can help ensure that your content is aligned with your business objectives and resonates with your target audience.

Potential Prompt: "How do you currently plan and create content for your website and social media channels, and how do you measure the effectiveness of your content?"

Benefit: A clear content strategy and calendar can help improve the consistency and quality of your content, attract more traffic to your website, and increase engagement with your target audience.

Challenge: **No unified posting strategy, schedule, or social media profile dashboard**

Fraserism: Develop a posting strategy and daily schedule that outlines the types of content you will post, the frequency of your posts, and the platforms you will use. This can help ensure that your social media presence is consistent and engaging.

Potential Prompt: "How do you currently plan and schedule your social media posts, and how do you measure the effectiveness of your social media presence?"

Benefit: A clear posting strategy and schedule in addition to managing all your social media platforms can help increase engagement with your target audience on social media, build brand awareness, and drive traffic to your website.

Challenge: **Without automation, lead generation and prospecting can be time-consuming**

Fraserism: Implement marketing automation tools that can help automate your lead generation and prospecting efforts, such as email campaigns and targeted ads. This can help save time and improve the efficiency of your sales and marketing efforts.

Potential Prompt: "How do you currently generate leads and prospects, and how do you manage and track these efforts?"

Benefit: Marketing automation can help increase the efficiency and effectiveness of your lead generation and prospecting efforts, allowing you to focus on high-priority activities and increase conversions.

Challenge: **image, video & webinar production and marketing can be time-consuming**

Fraserism: Implement video, image and webinar production and marketing automation tools that can help automate aspects of your video production and marketing, such as video editing and distribution. This can help save time and improve the efficiency of your video marketing efforts.

Potential Prompt: "How do you currently create and distribute videos for your marketing efforts, and how do you measure the effectiveness of your videos?"

Benefit: Video marketing automation can help improve the efficiency and effectiveness of your video marketing efforts, allowing you to reach a wider audience and increase engagement with your target audience.

Q. Dop you have an automated sales and marketing platform? Do you use AI to help you to streamline and automate your sales and marketing? Do you use AI to help you gain clarity, vision, and purpose to embrace, create and live your vision?

1. Yes. All done, planned, documented & executed by AI.
2. On the case. Working towards it, documenting it.
3. Oops. No, not yet completed (or started).
4. This is all too overwhelming. I Need help with this – fast.

You Could Replace All of These with Just One Solution...

Sales & Selling

Sales and selling are crucial components of any successful business. Maximizing sales and revenue is important for the growth and sustainability of your business whether you lease a building or work from home. To achieve your financial goals and objectives, have a well-defined sales process and if possible, an automated sales process, this can be a game changer for you.

A well-defined sales process streamlines and simplifies the sales process by leveraging technology and AI by reducing and eliminating manual tasks. This allows sales teams to focus on more important tasks such as building relationships with customers and closing deals.

An automated sales process can also lead to increased sales productivity and efficiency. It can help sales teams identify leads, track customer interactions, and manage sales pipelines more effectively. By automating tasks such as lead scoring and nurturing, companies can improve the quality of their leads and increase the likelihood of converting them into customers.

Furthermore, an automated sales process can provide valuable insights into customer behavior and sales performance. By tracking and analyzing data, companies can identify trends and patterns leading to new sales opportunities that can create responsive sales strategies and tactics. This data can also be used to improve customer experience and engagement resulting in more sales, larger opening orders, increased customer loyalty and extending the lifetime of a customer.

A well-defined and streamlined sales process is crucial for maximizing sales and revenue. By streamlining tasks and leveraging technology and AI, companies can improve sales productivity, efficiency, and performance whilst reducing churn. It is an essential tool for any business looking to stay competitive and grow in today's market.

Q. How many sales do you need to generate the revenue you want? ☐

Each of the points below are split into 4 parts.

- **Challenge:** common issue or obstacle often faced by business owners
- **Fraserism:** a helpful hint, tip, quote, or suggestion to help you in overcoming a challenge.
- **Potential Prompt:** a question, task, and prompt to ask your preferred ai-powered VA.
- **Benefit:** The potential benefit of researching, documenting, executing, automating, and refining a task, process, procedure, or workflow that addresses the underlying challenge.

Challenge: **No written sales plan document or strategy**
Fraserism: Create a written sales plan document that outlines your sales goals, target market, sales strategies, and action steps.
Potential Prompt: What are the key components of a successful sales plan document?
Benefit: Having a written sales plan document can help you stay focused, organized, and accountable for achieving your sales goals.

Challenge: **Without a sales team, you may be limited in your capacity to generate sales**
Fraserism: Build a sales team that is aligned with your sales goals, has the right skillset, and is committed to your sales process.
Potential Prompt: What are some best practices for building a successful sales team?
Benefit: Having a sales team can help you generate and close more sales, increase revenue, and improve overall sales performance.

Challenge: **Without a specific selling "system" or process, you may achieve your goals**
Fraserism: Develop and follow a specific selling system or process that is tailored to your target market and aligns with your sales goals.
Potential Prompt: What are some key components of an effective

selling system or process?

Benefit: Having a specific selling system or process can help you improve sales productivity, efficiency, and performance, as well as ensure a consistent and effective approach to selling.

Challenge: **To effectively communicate the value of your products or services to clients.**

Fraserism: Develop a sales presentation that highlights the key features and benefits of your products or services and highlights their value to prospective clients.

Potential Prompt: What are some best practices for creating an effective sales presentation?

Benefit: Having a sales presentation can help you effectively communicate the value of your products or services to prospective clients and increase the likelihood of closing a sale.

Challenge: **Not quantifying the financial impact of prospective client's problems & pain**

Fraserism: Use financial analysis tools to quantify the potential financial impact of your products or services on the prospective client's business, and effectively communicate this impact in your sales conversations.

Potential Prompt: How can I effectively quantify the financial impact of my products or services to prospective clients?

Benefit: Quantifying the financial impact of your products or services can help you effectively address prospective clients' concerns, highlight the value of your offerings, and increase the likelihood of closing a sale.

Challenge: **Leaving the "money" and asking for the order until the end of your appointment**

Fraserism: Make sure to ask for the order at the appropriate time during your appointment and be proactive in addressing any objections or concerns the prospect may have.

Potential Prompt: What are some best practices for asking for the order and closing a sale?

Benefit: Asking for the order at the appropriate time and proactively addressing objections or concerns can help you increase the likelihood of closing a sale and maximize revenue.

Challenge: **Not generating enough new prospects**
Fraserism: Develop and implement effective lead generation strategies that align with your target market and sales goals.
Potential Prompt: What are some effective lead generation strategies for my target market?
Benefit: Generating enough new prospects who are interested in your services can help you maintain a consistent flow of sales opportunities and

Challenge: **Many businesses struggle to follow up effectively with potential clients**
Fraserism: Use a customer relationship management (CRM) system to automate follow-up processes, such as sending personalized emails, setting reminders for follow-up calls, and scheduling appointments.
Potential Prompt: "Can you recommend a CRM system that would be suitable for automating our follow-up processes?"
Benefit: An automated follow-up system can save time and effort, improve communication with potential clients, and increase the chances of closing deals.

Challenge: **Not streamlining the steps in your sales process**
Fraserism: Map out the stages of your sales process, from prospecting to closing deals, and identify the specific actions that need to be taken at each stage.
Potential Prompt: "How can I create a visual representation of the sales process we use, and identify the specific actions we need to take at each stage?"
Benefit: Understanding the steps in your sales process can help you optimize your efforts, identify areas for improvement, and increase your chances of success.

Challenge: **Negotiating pricing without discounting can be difficult**
Fraserism: Identify value-added items that you can offer, such as free trials, discounts, or bundled packages, which can make your offer more attractive to potential clients.
Potential Prompt: "What are some additional items we could offer to sweeten the deal and make our offer more attractive to potential

clients?"

Benefit: Having additional value-added items to offer can help close deals and increase revenue, while also providing additional benefits to clients.

Challenge: **No clear understanding of the revenue targets**

Fraserism: Set clear revenue targets and identify the number of sales needed to achieve those targets, based on your historical conversion rates and average deal sizes.

Potential Prompt: "How can I determine the number of sales we need to achieve our revenue targets, and adjust our sales strategy accordingly?"

Benefit: Having clear revenue targets and sales goals can help focus sales efforts, prioritize activities, and increase the chances of achieving revenue targets.

Challenge: **No clear understanding of the number of leads needed to achieve revenue targets**

Fraserism: Determine the number of leads needed to achieve revenue targets, based on historical conversion rates and average deal sizes.

Potential Prompt: "How can I calculate the number of leads we need to achieve our revenue targets, and adjust our lead generation strategies accordingly?"

Benefit: Knowing the number of leads needed to achieve revenue targets can help focus lead generation efforts, prioritize activities, and increase the chances of achieving revenue targets.

Challenge: **No clear definition of what constitutes a lead or a prospect**

Fraserism: Define what a lead means to your business, including specific criteria and lead scoring such as demographics, behavior, and level of engagement.

Potential Prompt: "How can I create a clear definition of what a lead means to our business, can you please share an example lead scoring methodology I can use in my business?"

Benefit: Having a clear definition of what a lead is can help prioritize lead generation efforts, improve lead management, and increase the quality

Q. Are you generating the sales and revenue you need? Do you use AI to help you to streamline and automate your sales process? Do you use AI to help you gain clarity, vision, and purpose to embrace, create and live your vision?

1. Yes. All done, planned, documented & executed by AI.
2. On the case. Working towards it, documenting it.
3. Oops. No, not yet completed (or started).
4. This is all too overwhelming. I Need help with this – fast.

Borders was a major bookstore chain with a peak revenue of
$4.1 billion in 2006 and over 32,000
employees. However, Borders failed to adapt to the rise of
e-books and the changing reading habits of customers.

Competitors like Amazon and Barnes & Noble were able to
offer better prices, greater selection, and more convenient
digital delivery. Despite attempts to revamp their online
presence and offer e-books, Borders was unable to keep up
and filed for bankruptcy in 2011, leading to the closure of all its stores.

Get AI-powered help to save time, money & stress to do the
jobs you hate, don't have time for, or simply don't want to do.

Reduce costs, improve efficiency & ROI to achieve your
goals & objectives. It's your business. you're in control.
You make the decisions.

You decide what you want to achieve next.

Sales Territory

Effectively managing your sales territories is like playing a game of chess. Each chess piece has its own unique set of moves and abilities, just like each sales representative has their own set of skills and strategies. By assigning specific territories to each sales representative, you're essentially placing each piece on the chessboard, with the goal of capturing the most valuable pieces (i.e., sales opportunities).

Effective sales territory management involves dividing your target market into smaller, more manageable sections. Think of it like a pie that you're slicing into smaller pieces. Each slice is then assigned to a specific sales representative who is responsible for developing and executing a sales strategy within that area. This approach helps ensure that customers are being serviced in a consistent and efficient manner, while also allowing sales representatives to focus their efforts on specific areas rather than spreading themselves too thin.

By utilizing sales territory management, companies can reap numerous benefits. For instance, it allows for better resource allocation, as sales representatives can focus on the areas that are most likely to generate revenue. It also enables companies to identify untapped market opportunities that might have otherwise gone unnoticed. Additionally, by analyzing the performance of each territory using salesforce.com or LinkedIn's Sales Navigator, companies can make informed decisions about where to allocate resources and how to adjust their sales strategies.

In short, effective sales territory management is essential for identifying and maximizing sales opportunities and growth. Just like in a game of chess, it's all about strategic planning and making the most of your available resources to capture the most valuable pieces. By implementing a well-defined and managed sales territory system, companies can improve customer engagement, increase revenue, and optimize their overall sales performance.

Ultimately, investing in human resources and culture is essential for sustained success in today's competitive marketplace. By creating a positive work environment and complying with employment legislation, businesses can attract top talent, retain employees, and achieve long-term success.

Q. How many potential sales opportunities exist in your local, regional, and national territory? □

Each of the points below are split into 4 parts.

- **Challenge:** common issue or obstacle often faced by business owners
- **Fraserism:** a helpful hint, tip, quote, or suggestion to help you in overcoming a challenge.
- **Potential Prompt:** a question, task, and prompt to ask your preferred ai-powered VA.
- **Benefit:** The potential benefit of researching, documenting, executing, automating, and refining a task, process, procedure, or workflow that addresses the underlying challenge.

Challenge: **Lack of information about the sales territory**
Fraserism: Conduct a thorough analysis of the sales territory to determine the number of suspects and their potential value.
Potential Prompt: "How can we conduct a thorough analysis of our sales territory to determine the number of suspects and their potential value?"
Benefit: A thorough analysis of the sales territory can help you prioritize your efforts and focus on the most valuable prospects.

Challenge: **Lack of knowledge about the value of each sales territory.**
Fraserism: Determine the value of each sales territory by analyzing historical sales data and projecting future growth potential.
Potential Prompt: "How can we determine the value of each sales territory, and how can we use this information to prioritize our efforts?"

Benefit: Knowing the value of each sales territory can help you allocate resources effectively and maximize revenue potential.

Typical challenge: **Lack of information about competitors in each sales territory.**
Fraserism: Conduct a competitive analysis to identify the competitors in each sales territory and their strengths and weaknesses.
Potential Prompt: "How can we conduct a competitive analysis to identify our competitors in each sales territory and their strengths and weaknesses?"
Benefit: Knowing your competitors can help you differentiate your offering and develop strategies to win business.

Typical challenge: **Losing business within each sales territory due to lack of visibility.**
Fraserism: Conduct a win-loss analysis to understand why business is being lost and develop strategies to address the issues.
Potential Prompt: "How can we conduct a win-loss analysis to understand why we are losing business within each sales territory and develop strategies to address the issues?"
Benefit: Understanding why business is being lost can help you make improvements to your offering and processes and win more business.

Typical challenge: **Inability to generate enough new prospects who are interested in you.**
Fraserism: Develop a targeted prospecting strategy that leverages multiple channels and tactics.
Potential Prompt: "How can we develop a targeted prospecting strategy that leverages multiple channels and tactics to generate more interest in our services?"
Benefit: A targeted prospecting strategy can help you reach more qualified prospects and increase the likelihood of conversion.

Typical challenge: **Inability to close enough prospects and convert enough sales/revenue.**
Fraserism: Develop a sales process that is aligned with your target customer's buying process and provides clear next steps.
Potential Prompt: "How can we develop a sales process that is aligned with our target customer's buying process and provides clear

next steps to increase our conversion rates?"
Benefit: A clear and effective sales process can help you close more deals and generate more revenue.

Challenge: **Not understanding why customers choose competitors over you**
Fraserism: Conduct research to determine the top reasons why customers choose competitors over your business. Once identified, develop strategies to address those areas and improve your offerings.
Potential Prompt: "What are the top reasons why customers in our territory choose our competitors over us? How can we address those areas and improve our offerings?"
Benefit: Understanding the reasons why customers choose competitors over you can help you improve and refine your offerings and win more business in the long run.

Challenge: **Not understanding the top reasons why customers choose to do business with you**
Fraserism: Conduct research to determine the top reasons why customers choose to do business with you. Leverage those strengths to differentiate oneself from competitors and win more business.
Potential Prompt: "What are the top reasons why customers in our territory choose to do business with us? How can we leverage those strengths to differentiate ourselves from competitors and win more business?"
Benefit: Understanding the top reasons why customers choose to do business with you can help you differentiate yourself from competitors and win more business eventually.

Challenge: **Failing to track prospecting and sales activities daily**
Fraserism: Create a system to track and analyze prospecting and sales activities daily. Use the data to identify areas for improvement and adjust your strategies accordingly.
Potential Prompt: "Do we have a system in place to track and analyze our daily prospecting and sales activities? How can we use this data to identify areas for improvement and adjust our strategies accordingly?"
Benefit: Tracking prospecting and sales activities daily can help you identify areas for improvement and adjust your strategies to improve

and grow your business.

Challenge: **Not understanding the top objectives, you need to achieve to grow your territory**

Fraserism: Determine the top objectives you need to achieve to grow your territory and develop a strategic plan to achieve those objectives.

Potential Prompt: "What are the top objectives we need to achieve to grow our territory? How can we develop a strategic plan to achieve those objectives?"

Benefit: Understanding the top objectives, you need to achieve to grow your territory can help you develop a strategic plan to achieve those objectives and improve your chances of success.

Challenge: **Failing to identify and address the top problems in your territory**

Fraserism: Identify the top problems in your territory and develop strategies to address them, to improve your business and grow your territory.

Potential Prompt: "What are the top problems we need to address in our territory? How can we develop strategies to address those problems and improve our business?"

Benefit: Identifying and addressing the top problems in your territory can help you improve your business and grow your territory more efficiently and effectively.

Challenge: **Failing to offer value added items to increase or reduce the price**

Fraserism: Develop value added items that you can offer to increase the perceived value of your offerings, and/or reduce the price to make them more competitive.

Potential Prompt: "How can we develop value added items that we can offer to increase the perceived value of our offerings, and/or reduce the price to make them more competitive?"

Benefit: Offering value added items can help increase the perceived value of your offerings, make them more competitive, and improve your ability to win

Q. Are you generating the sales you want from specific territories? Do you use AI to help you to streamline and automate your sales process? Do you use AI to help you gain clarity, vision, and purpose to embrace, create and live your vision?

1. Yes. All done, planned, documented & executed by AI.
2. On the case. Working towards it, documenting it.
3. Oops. No, not yet completed (or started).
4. This is all too overwhelming. I Need help with this – fast.

Cashflow

Managing cash flow effectively is essential for any business to not only survive but also thrive. It involves carefully analyzing revenue streams, closely monitoring expenses, and forecasting future cash needs. Without a proper cash flow management plan in place, businesses may find themselves unable to pay bills, cover payroll, or pursue growth opportunities.

To effectively manage cash flow and revenue streams, businesses can identify areas for improvement and implement strategies to increase revenue and reduce costs. For instance, they can evaluate pricing strategies, explore additional revenue streams, streamline collections processes, and negotiate better payment terms with vendors.

Continually improving cash flow and revenue streams is beneficial not just during periods of growth but also during tough times, such as economic downturns or unexpected challenges. A strong cash flow position enables businesses to better manage cash shortages and respond to unexpected expenses.

Overall, effective cash flow management and revenue stream optimization are crucial for the long-term success and sustainability of any business. By maintaining a healthy cash flow, businesses can remain financially stable and invest in future growth opportunities.

Q. What is your current cost per lead, cost per sale & lifetime value of a customer? ☐

Each of the points below are split into 4 parts.

- **Challenge:** common issue or obstacle often faced by business owners
- **Fraserism:** a helpful hint, tip, quote, or suggestion to help you in overcoming a challenge.
- **Potential Prompt:** a question, task, and prompt to ask your

preferred ai-powered VA.

- **Benefit:** The potential benefit of researching, documenting, executing, automating, and refining a task, process, procedure, or workflow that addresses the underlying challenge.

Challenge: **Not having a written credit policy**
Fraserism: It is recommended to have a written credit policy that clearly outlines credit terms, credit limits, late payment penalties, and credit assessment procedures.
Potential Prompt: What are the steps involved in creating a written credit policy?
Benefit: Having a written credit policy can provide consistency in credit practices, reduce the risk of bad debt, and ensure that clients are aware of credit terms and procedures.

Challenge: **Not having a terms of business document**
Fraserism: It is recommended to have written terms of business document that outlines the scope of services, payment terms, responsibilities of both parties, and dispute resolution procedures.
Potential Prompt: What are some key elements to include in a terms of business document?
Benefit: Having a terms of business document can help clarify expectations and responsibilities for both parties, reduce misunderstandings, and minimize the risk of disputes.

Challenge: **Not having a credit application form**
Fraserism: It is recommended to use a credit application form to collect detailed information about new clients, including their business name, address, financial information, and references.
Potential Prompt: What are some key questions to include in a credit application form?
Benefit: Using a credit application form can help ensure that all necessary information is collected before extending credit, reduce the risk of bad debt, and provide a basis for credit assessment.

Challenge: **Not performing credit checks on new client accounts**
Fraserism: It is recommended to perform credit checks on new clients to assess their creditworthiness and determine appropriate credit

limits.

Potential Prompt: What are some sources for obtaining credit reports on new clients?

Benefit: Performing credit checks can help reduce the risk of bad debt, ensure that appropriate credit limits are set, and provide a basis for credit decisions.

Challenge: **Not having credit limits on new client accounts**

Fraserism: It is recommended to set credit limits for new clients based on their creditworthiness, payment history, and financial stability.

Potential Prompt: How can credit limits be determined for new clients?

Benefit: Setting credit limits can help reduce the risk of bad debt, ensure that credit exposure is managed effectively, and provide a basis for credit decisions.

Challenge: **Not providing credit assessment, collection, or legal procedures training for staff**

Fraserism: It is recommended to provide training to staff involved in credit assessment, collection, or legal procedures to ensure that credit practices are consistent and effective.

Potential Prompt: What are some key topics to cover in credit management training for staff?

Benefit: Providing training can help ensure that credit practices are consistent, reduce the risk of bad debt, and increase staff competence and confidence in credit management.

Challenge: **Not producing an aged debtor report monthly**

Fraserism: It is recommended to produce an aged debtor report monthly to identify overdue accounts and take appropriate collection action.

Potential Prompt: How can an aged debtor report be used to improve credit management practices?

Benefit: Producing an aged debtor report can help identify overdue accounts, improve collection practices, and reduce the risk of bad debt.

Challenge: **Not knowing if your credit terms are competitive**

Fraserism: Research the credit terms offered by competitors in your industry and adjust your credit terms accordingly to remain competitive.

Potential Prompt: "Have you ever researched the credit terms offered by your competitors? If not, I suggest looking into their terms to see if you are offering competitive credit terms."

Benefit: By adjusting your credit terms to remain competitive, you can potentially increase sales and maintain your market share.

Challenge: **When your product or service costs more than competitors**

Fraserism: Review your pricing strategy to ensure that it is competitive with other businesses in your industry. Consider offering promotions or discounts to offset any pricing disadvantages.

Potential Prompt: "Are you aware of the prices of your competitors? It may be worth reviewing your pricing strategy to ensure that your prices are competitive."

Benefit: By offering competitive prices, you can attract and retain more customers, increasing your revenue.

Challenge: **Not knowing the cost of extending credit to customers**

Fraserism: Calculate the cost of extending credit to customers by factoring in interest rates, late payment fees, and any expenses related to credit management.

Potential Prompt: "Do you know how much it costs your company to extend credit to customers? It may be worth calculating to ensure that you are managing your cash flow effectively."

Benefit: Understanding the cost of extending credit can help you make informed decisions about credit policies and cash flow management.

Challenge: **Poor invoice and statement management can result in additional costs.**

Fraserism: Calculate the cost of administering invoices and statements by factoring in the time and resources required for processing and delivery.

Potential Prompt: "Have you calculated the cost of administering invoices and statements? Knowing these costs can help you identify areas where you can streamline your invoicing and statement management processes."

Benefit: By streamlining your invoicing and statement management processes, you can reduce costs and improve cash flow management.

Challenge: **Collection efforts can be time-consuming and expensive**
Fraserism: Calculate the cost of collection efforts by factoring in the time and resources required for sending collection letters and making collection calls.
Potential Prompt: "Do you know the cost of your collection efforts? Knowing these costs can help you identify areas where you can improve your debt management processes."
Benefit: By improving debt management processes, you can reduce costs and improve cash flow management.

Challenge: **Not understanding your accounting fees can result in unexpected expenses**
Fraserism: Review your accounting fees and consider negotiating lower rates or finding more cost-effective accounting solutions.
Potential Prompt: "Have you reviewed your accounting fees recently? It may be worth exploring more cost-effective accounting solutions to reduce expenses."

Benefit: By reducing accounting fees, you can improve cash flow management and reduce expenses.

 Q. Dop you have an automated sales and marketing platform? Do you use AI to help you to streamline and automate your sales and marketing? Do you use AI to help you gain clarity, vision, and purpose to embrace, create and live your vision?

1. Yes. All done, planned, documented & executed by AI.
2. On the case. Working towards it, documenting it.
3. Oops. No, not yet completed (or started).
4. This is all too overwhelming. I Need help with this –

fast.

Advertising

Advertising is crucial for businesses to increase brand awareness, attract new customers, and drive sales. Both online and offline advertising can be effective, depending on the business's goals and target audience.

Online advertising, such as social media ads and Google Ads, has become increasingly popular due to its ability to target specific audiences and its cost-effectiveness. For example, a sports equipment company might use targeted Facebook ads to reach people who have shown an interest in sports. By targeting the right audience, businesses can increase the likelihood of reaching potential customers who are more likely to convert.

However, offline advertising, such as billboards, print ads, and television commercials, can still be effective in reaching a wider audience and establishing brand credibility. For instance, a luxury car company might use a billboard in a high-traffic area to increase brand awareness among a broader audience.

To ensure that advertising efforts are efficient and effective, businesses should focus on maximizing the Return on Advertising Spend (ROAS) and minimizing marketing acquisition costs. Maximizing ROAS involves generating a positive return on investment by creating compelling ad content and continuously optimizing ad campaigns based on performance data. For example, a clothing company might analyze which ad campaigns generate the most sales and allocate more resources to those campaigns.

Minimizing marketing acquisition costs involves reducing the amount of money spent on acquiring new customers by improving customer retention and increasing customer referrals. For example, a subscription-based service might offer discounts to current customers who refer friends to the service.

In conclusion, both online and offline advertising are important for businesses to reach their target audience and drive sales. By maximizing ROAS and minimizing marketing acquisition costs, businesses can ensure that their advertising efforts are efficient and effective, allowing them to allocate more resources towards other important areas of the business.

Q. Do you advertise in FREE newspapers, trade journals or online platforms? ☐

Each of the points below are split into 4 parts.

- **Challenge:** common issue or obstacle often faced by business owners
- **Fraserism:** a helpful hint, tip, quote, or suggestion to help you in overcoming a challenge.
- **Potential Prompt:** a question, task, and prompt to ask your preferred ai-powered VA.
- **Benefit:** The potential benefit of researching, documenting, executing, automating, and refining a task, process, procedure, or workflow that addresses the underlying challenge.

Challenge: **Not running any online advertising campaigns on TikTok, YouTube, Google Ads.**
Fraserism: I recommend that you explore running online advertising campaigns on TikTok, YouTube, Google Ads or Bing Ads as these platforms have large user bases and offer various targeting options to reach your desired audience. For instance, TikTok has over 1 billion active users and its algorithm enables advertisers to target users based on interests, location, gender, age, and more.
Potential Prompt: Can you share some insights on how we can reach younger audiences and increase our brand's online visibility?
Benefit: Running online advertising campaigns on these platforms can help you reach a wider audience and increase brand visibility, leading to potential increases in website traffic and sales.

Challenge: **Not advertising on social media platforms such as Facebook, Instagram, or Twitter.**

Fraserism: I suggest that you consider advertising on social media platforms such as Facebook, Instagram, or Twitter as they offer advanced targeting options, including demographic, geographic, and interest-based targeting. For example, Facebook's Ads Manager allows you to create custom audiences based on users' interests, behaviors, and demographics.

Potential Prompt: Can you recommend a social media platform where we can reach our target audience of tech-savvy millennials who enjoy outdoor activities?

Benefit: Advertising on social media platforms can help you reach a highly targeted audience, increase engagement with your brand, and drive conversions.

Challenge: **Not considered using programmatic advertising to target specific audiences.**

Fraserism: I recommend exploring programmatic advertising to reach specific audiences, as it enables you to deliver targeted ads to the right people at the right time. Programmatic advertising uses data to automate ad buying, allowing you to reach your desired audience with precision.

Potential Prompt: Can you share some insights on how programmatic advertising can help us reach our target audience more effectively than traditional advertising methods?

Benefit: Programmatic advertising can help you reach a highly targeted audience, increase ad relevance and engagement, and optimize your advertising spend.

Challenge: **Not running any display advertising campaigns on websites or apps.**

Fraserism: I recommend that you consider running display advertising campaigns on websites or apps as they offer a wide range of targeting options and ad formats. For example, Google Display Network allows you to target users based on their interests, demographics, and behaviors, and offers various ad formats such as text, image, and video ads.

Potential Prompt: Can you recommend a display advertising strategy that will help us increase brand awareness and engagement?

Benefit: Running display advertising campaigns can help you reach a wider audience and increase brand awareness, leading to potential increases in website traffic and sales.

Challenge: Not tried advertising on video platforms such as YouTube or Vimeo.

Fraserism: I recommend exploring advertising on video platforms such as YouTube or Vimeo, as they offer various ad formats, including pre-roll, mid-roll, and post-roll ads, and can reach a large audience. For instance, YouTube has over 2 billion monthly active users and offers various targeting options, including demographic, geographic, and interest-based targeting.

Potential Prompt: Can you recommend a video advertising strategy that will help us increase brand awareness and engagement on YouTube?

Benefit: Advertising on video platforms can help you reach a highly engaged audience, increase brand awareness and engagement, and drive conversions.

Challenge: Not determined your target audience for your online and offline advertising.

Fraserism: Conduct market research to identify your target audience and their preferences. Use this information to tailor your advertising campaigns to better reach and resonate with your desired audience.

Potential Prompt: "What methods do you use to identify and target your ideal audience in your advertising campaigns?"

Benefit: Identifying and targeting your ideal audience can lead to higher engagement rates and result in a greater return on advertising spend (ROAS).

Challenge: Not advertising in local, regional, or weekly free newspapers.

Fraserism: Consider diversifying your advertising channels by investing in digital advertising methods, such as social media advertising, search engine advertising, or programmatic advertising. These methods can offer more precise targeting options and provide valuable data to measure the success of your campaigns.

Potential Prompt: "What digital advertising methods have you explored to complement your offline advertising efforts?"

Benefit: Diversifying your advertising channels can help increase your brand's visibility and reach while providing a better understanding of your target audience's behavior and preferences.

Challenge: **Not set a budget for your online and offline advertising campaigns.**
Fraserism: Develop a comprehensive advertising budget based on your business goals, audience reach, and ROAS expectations. This will help ensure that your advertising efforts are cost-effective and that you're not overspending on campaigns that aren't providing a return on investment.
Potential Prompt: "How do you determine the appropriate budget for your advertising campaigns and how do you measure the ROAS?"
Benefit: Setting a realistic advertising budget can help you allocate resources effectively and maximize the ROI of your advertising efforts.

Challenge: **Not established metrics to measure the success of your advertising campaigns.**
Fraserism: Identify and track key performance indicators (KPIs) such as website traffic, lead generation, conversions, or brand awareness. These metrics can help you understand the effectiveness of your advertising campaigns and optimize them accordingly.
Potential Prompt: "What KPIs do you use to measure the success of your advertising campaigns, and how do you track and analyze these metrics?"
Benefit: Establishing clear KPIs and tracking your advertising campaigns' performance can help you optimize your campaigns for better results, leading to a higher ROAS.

Challenge: **Not tested different ad creatives and messaging for your advertising campaigns.**
Fraserism: Create multiple variations of ad creatives and messaging and conduct A/B tests to determine which ones resonate better with your target audience. This can help you optimize your campaigns and increase your ROAS.
Potential Prompt: "How often do you test different ad creatives and messaging, and what methods do you use to analyze the results?"
Benefit: A/B testing your ad creatives and messaging can help you identify what resonates with your target audience and optimize your campaigns for better results.

Challenge: **Not running your online and offline advertising campaigns frequently enough.**

Fraserism: Develop a consistent advertising schedule and frequency that aligns with your business goals and target audience preferences. This can help increase brand awareness and improve engagement rates, leading to a higher ROAS.

Potential Prompt: "How often do you run your advertising campaigns, and how do you determine the optimal frequency to maximize your ROAS?"

Benefit: Consistently running your advertising campaigns can help increase your brand's visibility and reach, leading to a higher ROAS.

Challenge: **Not advertising in exhibition, trade show and expo guides and catalogues**

Fraserism: Consider advertising in tradeshow, expo and exhibition guides and catalogues to increase brand visibility among attendees. This can involve purchasing ad space in event materials, such as printed programs or online listings, or sponsoring a booth or exhibit at the event. For example, you could ask the event organizers about advertising opportunities and the costs involved.

Benefit: Advertising in exhibitions, trade show and expo guides and catalogues can increase brand awareness and lead to more sales from attendees who are interested in your products or services. By promoting your brand at events, you can also build relationships with other businesses in your industry and generate potential leads for future partnerships.

Challenge: **Not advertising on vehicles, buses, or taxis**

Fraserism: Consider advertising on vehicles, buses, or taxis to increase your brand visibility in high-traffic areas. This can involve wrapping a vehicle or bus with your brand messaging or placing ads on the sides of taxis. For example, you could contact a local advertising agency that specializes in vehicle wraps or taxi advertising.

Benefit: Advertising on vehicles, buses or taxis may help you reach a large audience that may not be exposed to your brand through other marketing channels. This form of advertising can be highly targeted and cost-effective, as it allows you to reach specific demographics or geographic areas. In addition, vehicle advertising can increase brand recognition and recall, as people tend to remember eye-catching and creative ads on the move.

Challenge: **Not advertising at schools, colleges, or universities**
Fraserism: Consider advertising at schools, colleges, or universities to increase brand awareness and reach potential customers within the campus community. This can involve placing ads in school newspapers or on bulletin boards, sponsoring campus events or activities, or partnering with student organizations. For example, you could contact the school's marketing or advertising department to inquire about advertising opportunities.
Benefit: Advertising at schools, colleges or universities can help you reach a highly targeted audience of students and faculty who may be interested in your products or services. This form of advertising can also help you build relationships with schools or institutions and create opportunities for future collaborations or partnerships. Additionally, advertising in school newspapers or on bulletin boards can be cost-effective and offer a high return on investment.

Challenge: **Not advertising on other people's websites**
Fraserism: Consider advertising on other people's websites to increase brand visibility and drive traffic to your own website. This can involve purchasing banner ads, sponsored posts or sponsored content on relevant websites or blogs. For example, you could use Google Ads or other online advertising platforms to target specific websites or audiences.
Benefit: Advertising on other people's websites can help you reach a larger audience that may not be exposed to your brand through other marketing channels. This form of advertising can also help you build relationships with other businesses or websites in your industry and generate potential leads for future collaborations or partnerships. Additionally, advertising on relevant websites or blogs can drive targeted traffic to your own website and increase conversions.

 Q. Are you considering advertising your products, services, or solutions? Do you use AI to help you to better manage your online advertising as it can be

212

very confusing, overwhelming and time consuming? Do you use AI to help you gain clarity, vision, and purpose to embrace, create and live your vision?

1. Yes. All done, planned, documented & implemented in the business.
2. On the case. Working towards it, documenting it.
3. Oops. No, not yet completed (or started).
4. This is all too overwhelming. I Need help with this – fast.

CRM

Customer Relationship Management, or CRM, is a powerful tool that helps businesses manage and analyze customer interactions and data. For example, Salesforce and HubSpot are two popular CRM solutions that businesses can use to track and analyze customer behavior, manage leads and sales pipelines, and improve communication with customers.

By using CRM, businesses can identify opportunities for upselling and cross-selling, which can increase revenue and strengthen customer relationships. For instance, if a customer has recently purchased a product, the business can use CRM data to suggest complementary products or services that might interest the customer.

Moreover, CRM helps businesses stay organized by centralizing customer data, tracking interactions, and automating tasks. This leads to improved efficiency and reduced workload, allowing businesses to focus on providing excellent customer service.

Overall, the benefits of using a CRM system are numerous. It can help businesses streamline their sales processes, improve customer relationships, and increase revenue. While it may take some time to master, with the right training and support, businesses can leverage the power of CRM to take their sales and customer service to new heights.

One thing is for sure, creating a streamlined, responsive, personalized, and automated customer journey is vital for any business that wants to stand out from the competition and build a loyal customer base. By doing so, businesses can not only meet but exceed their customers' expectations and reap the benefits of a successful customer experience.

Q. How do you manage your pipeline of sales leads? ☐

Each of the points below are split into 4 parts.

- **Challenge:** common issue or obstacle often faced by business owners
- **Fraserism:** a helpful hint, tip, quote, or suggestion to help you in overcoming a challenge.
- **Potential Prompt:** a question, task, and prompt to ask your preferred ai-powered VA.
- **Benefit:** The potential benefit of researching, documenting, executing, automating, and refining a task, process, procedure, or workflow that addresses the underlying challenge.

Challenge: **Inadequate organization and management of customer data.**
Fraserism: It is important to have a centralized database to manage customer information effectively.
Potential Prompt: How can I ensure that my data is managed efficiently in my CRM system?
Benefit: By having an organized and centralized customer database, businesses can easily access customer information, improve customer service, and increase customer retention.

Challenge: **Inability to track customer interactions and communication.**
Fraserism: Implement a system for tracking all customer interactions and communication to enhance customer engagement.
Potential Prompt: How can I track customer interactions and communication in my CRM system?
Benefit: By tracking customer interactions and communication, businesses can better understand their customers' needs and preferences and provide personalized customer experiences.

Challenge: **Lack of sales tracking capabilities.**
Fraserism: Implement sales tracking features in your CRM system to improve sales performance and identify sales trends.
Potential Prompt: How can I use my CRM system to track sales performance and identify sales trends?

Benefit: By tracking sales performance and identifying sales trends, businesses can make informed decisions about sales strategies and increase revenue.

Challenge: **Inability to generate reports.**
Fraserism: Utilize reporting features in your CRM system to generate valuable insights and improve decision-making.
Potential Prompt: How can I use my CRM system to generate reports and gain insights about my business operations?
Benefit: By generating reports and gaining insights, businesses can identify areas for improvement and make data-driven decisions.

Challenge: **Insufficient customization to meet specific business needs.**
Fraserism: Customize your CRM system to meet the unique needs of your business.
Example Prompt: How can I customize my CRM system to meet the specific needs of my business?
Benefit: By customizing your CRM system, businesses can improve efficiency, streamline workflows, and enhance overall productivity.

Challenge: **Lack of clear customer segments and a well-defined ideal customer avatar**
Fraserism: Conduct thorough market research and analysis to identify customer needs and preferences and use that data to create detailed customer personas. Refine and update these profiles regularly based on customer feedback and new insights.
Potential Prompt: How do you currently determine which customers to target with your marketing and sales efforts?
Benefit: Having well-defined customer segments and an ideal customer profile can help you create more targeted and effective marketing campaigns, resulting in higher conversion rates and more loyal customers.

Challenge: **Setting clear and measurable goals is essential for effective CRM implementation**
Fraserism: Start by identifying your most pressing business challenges, such as low sales or poor customer retention rates, and use these as a starting point for setting CRM goals. Ensure that each

goal is specific, measurable, and achievable, and establish a clear process for tracking progress and adjusting as needed.

Potential Prompt: What are your current business goals, and how are you measuring progress towards achieving them?

Benefit: Clear and measurable CRM goals can help focus your team's efforts on key business priorities, while providing a benchmark for assessing performance and identifying areas for improvement.

Challenge: **Integrating your CRM system with social media networks**

Fraserism: Look for CRM solutions that offer robust integrations with a wide range of social media platforms and other business systems, such as email marketing tools and order processing software. Be sure to test each integration thoroughly before deployment to ensure that data is flowing correctly between systems.

Potential Prompt: What social media platforms are you currently using to engage with customers, and how are you tracking these interactions?

Benefit: Integrating your CRM with other business tools can help streamline workflows, reduce data entry errors, and improve customer engagement across multiple channels.

Challenge: **Limiting access to your CRM system to your sales team only**

Fraserism: Consider extending CRM access to other departments and teams, such as marketing, customer service, and accounting, to ensure that all relevant data is being captured and utilized. Implement robust security protocols to protect sensitive customer information from unauthorized access.

Potential Prompt: Who currently has access to your CRM system, and how is access managed and monitored?

Benefit: Broadening access to your CRM system can help increase visibility into customer interactions and behaviors, leading to more informed decision-making and improved business outcomes.

Challenge: **A lack of clarity around the steps in your sales process can result in confusion**

Fraserism: Develop a clear and well-defined sales process that maps out each step in the customer journey, from lead generation to closing the sale. Assign clear ownership and responsibilities for each step and establish metrics for tracking progress and assessing performance.

Example Prompt: How do you currently track and manage the various stages of your sales process?

Benefit: Having a well-defined sales process can help ensure that no leads fall through the cracks, while also enabling you to identify areas for improvement and optimize your sales efforts over time.

Challenge: **Uncertainty around the source of traffic and leads**

Fraserism: Implement tracking mechanisms, such as lead source codes, to capture information about where leads are coming from. Analyze this data regularly to identify trends and patterns and adjust your marketing efforts accordingly.

Potential Prompt: How do you currently track and analyze the source of your leads and prospects?

Benefit: Understanding where your leads come from can help you optimize your marketing efforts, reduce acquisition costs, and with better targeting – improve conversions.

Q. Dop you have an automated sales and marketing platform? Do you use AI to help you to streamline and automate your sales and marketing? Do you use AI to help you gain clarity, vision, and purpose to embrace, create and live your vision?

1. Yes. All done, planned, documented & executed by AI.

2. On the case. Working towards it, documenting it.

3. Oops. No, not yet completed (or started).

4. This is all too overwhelming. I Need help with this – fast.

Customer Journey

In today's competitive business landscape, providing customers with an exceptional experience is essential for success. Creating a streamlined, responsive, personalized, and automated customer journey can help businesses achieve just that.

Imagine walking into a physical store and having trouble finding what you're looking for. You try to ask a sales associate for help, but they're not responsive or available. Frustrating, right? The same applies to online experience - customers want to easily navigate through a business's website or app and receive timely assistance if needed.

Personalization is another crucial aspect of the customer's journey. Think about how it feels to receive an email or notification that's specifically tailored to your interests or past purchases. It feels like the business understands you and values your patronage.

Automation can also greatly enhance the customer experience. For example, imagine receiving a confirmation email immediately after placing an order, followed by regular updates on the status of your delivery. This saves time and reduces anxiety for customers, ensuring a positive experience.

A successful customer journey not only results in higher customer satisfaction and loyalty but can also lead to increased revenue and growth for the business. By understanding customers' needs and preferences, businesses can improve their offerings and attract new customers through positive word-of-mouth referrals.

In conclusion, creating a streamlined, responsive, personalized, and automated customer journey is vital for any business that wants to stand out from the competition and build a loyal customer base. By doing so, businesses can not only meet but exceed their customers' expectations and reap the benefits of a successful customer experience.

Q. How do you manage your pipeline of sales leads? ☐

Each of the points below are split into 4 parts.

- **Challenge:** common issue or obstacle often faced by business owners
- **Fraserism:** a helpful hint, tip, quote, or suggestion to help you in overcoming a challenge.
- **Potential Prompt:** a question, task, and prompt to ask your preferred ai-powered VA.
- **Benefit:** The potential benefit of researching, documenting, executing, automating, and refining a task, process, procedure, or workflow that addresses the underlying challenge.

Challenge: **Not fully understand your customers' needs and pain points**
Fraserism: Conduct market research and gather customer feedback to gain insights into their needs and pain points. Use this information to tailor your marketing and customer service efforts accordingly.
Potential Prompt: "What methods do you currently use to gather customer feedback?"
Benefit: By understanding your customers' needs and pain points, you can create a more effective and personalized customer journey, leading to increased customer satisfaction and loyalty.

Challenge: **Nott have a clear understanding of your customers' journey**
Fraserism: Map out your customers' journey and identify touchpoints where you can improve the customer experience.
Potential Prompt: "Can you walk me through the different stages of your customers' journey?"
Benefit: By understanding the customer journey, you can identify areas for improvement and create a more streamlined and effective customer experience.

Challenge: **Your marketing efforts may not be tailored to each stage of the customer journey**

Fraserism: Create targeted marketing campaigns for each stage of the customer journey, with personalized messaging and offers.
Potential Prompt: "How do you currently tailor your marketing efforts to different stages of the customer journey?"
Benefit: By creating targeted marketing campaigns, you can increase engagement and conversions throughout the customer journey.

Challenge: **Customers may have difficulty finding and purchasing your products/services**
Fraserism: Optimize your website and other sales channels to make it easy for customers to find and purchase your products/services.
Potential Prompt: "What steps have you taken to make it easy for customers to find and purchase your products/services?"
Benefit: By making it easy for customers to find and purchase your products/services, you can increase conversions and customer satisfaction.

Challenge: **You may not be providing personalized recommendations and offers**
Fraserism: Use customer data to provide personalized recommendations and offers based on their past behavior.
Potential Prompt: "How do you currently use customer data to personalize the customer experience?"
Benefit: By providing personalized recommendations and offers, you can increase customer engagement and loyalty.

Challenge: **Your customer service team may not be easily accessible and responsive**
Fraserism: Ensure that your customer service team is easily accessible and responsive through multiple channels, such as phone, email, and chat.
Potential Prompt: "What methods do you currently use to make your customer service team accessible and responsive?"
Benefit: By providing accessible and responsive customer service, you can increase customer satisfaction and loyalty.

Challenge: **Not be effectively collecting and using customer feedback**
Fraserism: Implement a system for collecting and using customer

feedback, such as surveys or customer feedback software. Use this feedback to improve the customer experience.

Potential Prompt: "How do you currently collect and use customer feedback to improve the customer experience?"

Benefit: By effectively using customer feedback, you can identify areas for improvement and create a more effective customer journey.

Challenge: **Not having a regular process for mapping out their customer journey.**

Fraserism: We recommend setting up a regular schedule for reviewing and mapping out the customer's journey, such as quarterly or bi-annually. This can involve gathering data from various sources, such as customer feedback, website analytics, and sales reports. For example, the prompt could be, "What process do you have in place for regularly reviewing and mapping out your customer journey?" The benefit of this prompt is that it can help identify any gaps or issues in the customer's journey that may have gone unnoticed and allow for improvements to be made in a timely manner.

Challenge: **Not having identified all touchpoints in their customer journey.**

Fraserism: We suggest conducting a comprehensive audit of all touchpoints, both digital and physical, to ensure that no touchpoints are missed. This can involve mapping out the customer's journey and identifying all interactions that a customer may have with the company. For example, prompt could be, "How have you identified all touchpoints in your customer journey?" The benefit of this prompt is that it can help ensure that all touchpoints are accounted for, leading to a more holistic and effective customer journey.

Challenge: **customer service representatives may not be trained to handle all stages**

Fraserism: We suggest providing comprehensive training to customer service representatives that covers all stages of the customer journey, including pre-purchase, purchase, and post-purchase interactions. This can involve creating training materials, providing ongoing support, and coaching. For example, prompt could be, "What training and support do you provide to customer service representatives to ensure they can handle all stages of the customer journey?" The benefit of this prompt is that it can help ensure that customer service representatives are equipped to provide excellent service throughout the customer's journey.

Challenge: **Not having a clear system for measuring customer satisfaction at each stage**
Fraserism: We recommend implementing a customer feedback system that allows customers to provide feedback at each touchpoint on the journey. This can involve using surveys, ratings, and reviews to gather customer feedback and track satisfaction metrics over time. For example, the prompt could be, "How do you measure customer satisfaction at each stage of the customer journey?" The benefit of this prompt is that it can help companies identify areas of the customer journey that are performing well, as well as areas that need improvement.

Challenge: **Having bottlenecks in their customer journey**
Fraserism: We suggest conducting a thorough analysis of the customer journey to identify any bottlenecks or areas of friction that may be causing delays or frustration for customers. This can involve using data analytics, customer feedback, and process mapping to identify areas for improvement. For example, prompt could be, "Have you identified any bottlenecks or areas of friction in your customer journey? If so, how are you addressing them?" The benefit of this prompt is that it can help companies improve the overall customer experience by addressing pain points and streamlining the customer journey.

Q. Dop you have an automated sales and marketing platform? Do you use AI to help you to streamline and automate your sales and marketing? Do you use AI to help you gain clarity, vision, and purpose to embrace, create and live your vision?

1. Yes. All done, planned, documented & executed by AI.

2. On the case. Working towards it, documenting it.

3. Oops. No, not yet completed (or started).

4. This is all too overwhelming. I Need help with this – fast.

Reporting Systems

Measuring progress and success is crucial for any organization, and clear Key Performance Indicators (KPIs) and accurate reporting systems are essential tools in this process. KPIs help organizations track and analyze their performance, identify areas for improvement, and make informed decisions. However, the effectiveness of KPIs is dependent on the accuracy of the data used to measure them.

Think of KPIs as the GPS of your organization. Just like a GPS system provides you with the most accurate and efficient route to your destination, KPIs provide you with a clear and reliable roadmap to success. But, just like a GPS system is only as good as the data it's using, KPIs are only as effective as the accuracy of the data used to measure them.

Having accurate reporting systems is essential to ensure that the data used to measure KPIs is reliable and up to date. These systems should be designed to provide timely and accurate information that is easily understandable by stakeholders, shareholders, and investors. Think of them like a dashboard in your car, providing you with real-time updates on your vehicle's performance, fuel consumption, and speed.

Many martech systems, analytics solutions, and accounting packages offer real-time reporting, providing a snapshot of key metrics on a single page. This allows senior management to quickly assess the organization's performance and make informed decisions.

Remember, defining clear KPIs and having accurate reporting systems is crucial for measuring confidence, progress, and success for stakeholders, shareholders, and investors. The more accurate the reporting, the better the insights for making informed decisions that will benefit the organization in the long term.

Q. What are your operating costs per month, and do you produce a monthly P&L? ☐

Each of the points below are split into 4 parts.

- **Challenge:** common issue or obstacle often faced by business owners
- **Fraserism:** a helpful hint, tip, quote, or suggestion to help you in overcoming a challenge.
- **Potential Prompt:** a question, task, and prompt to ask your preferred ai-powered VA.
- **Benefit:** The potential benefit of researching, documenting, executing, automating, and refining a task, process, procedure, or workflow that addresses the underlying challenge.

Challenge: **Not ahead of your financial projections for the year to date**
Fraserism: Review your financial projections for the year and identify areas where you can increase revenue and reduce expenses. Consider implementing cost-cutting measures and identifying new revenue streams. It may also be helpful to conduct a financial analysis to identify any inefficiencies or areas for improvement.
Potential Prompt: "What steps can I take to improve my financial performance for the year and meet my projections?"
Benefit: By identifying areas for improvement and implementing changes, you can increase revenue and improve profitability.

Challenge: **Not ahead of your financial projections for the quarter as per your sales plan.**
Fraserism: Review your sales plan and identify any areas where you can increase sales or reduce expenses. Consider implementing new sales strategies, expanding your target market, or adjusting your pricing strategy. It may also be helpful to conduct a sales analysis to identify any inefficiencies or areas for improvement.
Potential Prompt: "What steps can I take to improve my sales performance for the quarter and meet my projections?"
Benefit: By identifying areas for improvement and implementing changes, you can increase revenue and improve profitability.

Challenge: **Not generated more leads and new customers for the**

month as per your plan.

Fraserism: Review your marketing plan and identify any areas where you can increase your marketing efforts. Consider implementing new marketing strategies, expanding your target market, or adjusting your messaging. It may also be helpful to conduct a marketing analysis to identify any inefficiencies or areas for improvement.

Potential Prompt: "What steps can I take to improve my lead generation and customer acquisition for the month?"

Benefit: By increasing lead generation and customer acquisition, you can increase revenue and improve profitability.

Challenge: **You do not know how much money you owe and to whom.**

Fraserism: Implement an accurate and up-to-date accounting system to track your expenses and debts. It is important to maintain accurate records of all financial transactions and regularly reconcile your accounts to ensure accuracy.

Potential Prompt: "How can I improve my accounting and financial tracking to ensure that I know how much I owe and to whom?"

Benefit: By maintaining accurate financial records, you can better manage your debts and avoid financial complications.

Challenge: **You have not updated your terms and conditions in the last 6 months.**

Fraserism: Regularly review and update your terms and conditions to ensure that they reflect current legal and industry standards. This can help to protect your business from legal and financial risks.

Potential Prompt: "What steps can I take to update my terms and conditions to ensure that they are up-to-date and legally compliant?"

Benefit: By updating your terms and conditions, you can protect your business from legal and financial risks.

Challenge: **You do not know how much is owed to you and to whom.**

Fraserism: Implement an accurate and up-to-date accounting system to track your revenue and debts. It is important to maintain accurate records of all financial transactions and regularly reconcile your accounts to ensure accuracy.

Potential Prompt: "How can I improve my accounting and financial tracking to ensure that I know how much is owed to me and from whom?"

Benefit: By maintaining accurate financial records, you can better manage your revenue and debts and avoid financial complications.

Challenge: **You do not know how many signups you're generating daily.**

Solution: Use a tracking tool to monitor the number of signups daily, such as Google Analytics or a CRM with integrated reporting features. Set up alerts to notify you of any significant changes in signup numbers.

Potential Prompt: "Can you show me how many signups we generated yesterday?"

Benefit: Knowing the number of daily signups can help you evaluate the effectiveness of your marketing campaigns and make data-driven decisions to optimize your strategy.

Challenge: **You do not have a pipeline management or lead scoring tool.**

Solution: Implement a pipeline management tool and set up a lead scoring system to prioritize and segment leads based on their likelihood to convert. This can help your sales team focus on the most promising leads and improve conversion rates.

Potential Prompt: "Can you show me which leads are most likely to convert based on their lead score?"

Benefit: A pipeline management and lead scoring tool can help streamline your sales process, increase efficiency, and boost revenue.

Challenge: **You do not know how many visitors you're generating daily.**

Solution: Use a web analytics tool such as Google Analytics to track daily website traffic. Analyze trends and set up alerts to identify any significant changes in traffic.

Potential Prompt: "Can you show me how many visitors we had on our website yesterday?"

Benefit: Knowing the number of daily website visitors can help you track the effectiveness of your website and marketing efforts and make data-driven decisions to improve your online presence.

Challenge: **You do not know how many new inbound enquiries you're generating monthly.**

Solution: Set up a system to track and log all inbound enquiries, such as a CRM or dedicated email address. Use reporting tools to monitor the number of new enquiries on a monthly basis and analyze trends.

Potential Prompt: "Can you show me how many new enquiries we received last month?"

Benefit: Tracking the number of new enquiries can help you evaluate the effectiveness of your marketing campaigns and make data-driven decisions to optimize your strategy.

Challenge: **You do not know how many new proposals you are sending out monthly**

Solution: Use a CRM or project management tool to track the number of proposals sent out monthly. Set up alerts to notify you of any proposals that are outstanding or require follow-up.

Potential Prompt: "Can you show me how many proposals we sent out last month?"

Benefit: Tracking the number of proposals sent out can help you evaluate the effectiveness of your sales process and make data-driven decisions to improve conversion rates.

Challenge: **You do not know how many non-converted leads you have on your database**

Solution: Use a CRM or lead tracking tool to monitor the number of non-converted leads in your database. Analyze trends and identify areas for improvement in your sales process.

Potential Prompt: "Can you show me how many leads in our database have not yet converted?"

Benefit: Tracking the number of non-converted leads can help you identify areas for improvement in your sales process and make data-driven decisions to improve conversion rates.

Challenge: **You do not know your current cost per lead and cost per sale.**

Solution: Use CRM or accounting software to track the costs associated with generating leads and making sales. Calculate your cost per lead and cost per sale on a regular basis and analyze trends.

Potential Prompt: "Can you show me our current cost per lead and cost per sale?"

Benefit: Knowing your cost per lead and cost per sale can help you evaluate the effectiveness of your marketing and sales efforts and make data-driven decisions to optimize your strategy.

Q. Are you generating good insights and management reports? Do you use AI to help you to generate excellent reporting to spot new sales opportunities and opportunities for growth? Do you use AI to help you gain clarity, vision, and purpose to embrace, create and live your vision?

1. Yes. All done, planned, documented & implemented into our website.

2. On the case. Working towards it, documenting it.

3. Oops. No, not yet completed (or started).

4. This is all too overwhelming. I Need help with this – fast.

it
stacks
up

HIGH GROWTH

Leadership & Team Development

Successful businesses require a combination of good leadership, well-defined standard operating procedures (SOPs), and effective team development. Without these key components, it can be difficult to achieve and maintain success.

Effective leadership is crucial for any team to function at its best. Leaders who possess strong communication skills can inspire and motivate their team to work together towards a common goal. By delegating tasks and providing guidance, leaders can ensure that everyone is working towards the same objectives.

SOPs are important because they provide clear and concise instructions on how tasks should be performed. This ensures that everyone is on the same page and reduces the risk of errors, delays, and misunderstandings. SOPs also allow for consistency in the company's operations, which can help reduce inefficiencies and financial losses.

Team development is another critical component of business success. By investing in the development of their employees, businesses can improve productivity and work quality. Additionally, team development can foster trust and collaboration, leading to better communication and more effective problem-solving.

In summary, good leadership, SOPs, and team development are all essential components for business success. They must be reviewed and continuously improved to adapt to changes in the business environment and ensure ongoing effectiveness. By prioritizing these components, businesses can achieve their goals and maintain a competitive edge.

Q. How many people work for you in your business? ☐

Each of the points below are split into 4 parts.

- **Challenge:** common issue or obstacle often faced by business owners
- **Fraserism:** a helpful hint, tip, quote, or suggestion to help you in overcoming a challenge.
- **Potential Prompt:** a question, task, and prompt to ask your preferred ai-powered VA.
- **Benefit:** The potential benefit of researching, documenting, executing, automating, and refining a task, process, procedure, or workflow that addresses the underlying challenge.

Challenge: **No organizational chart or onboarding process**
Fraserism: Create an organizational chart and onboarding process to ensure new employees understand their role, responsibilities, and the company structure. Hold regular meetings with new employees to provide training and support.
Potential Prompt: What steps can I take to create an effective onboarding process for new employees?
Benefit: An effective onboarding process will increase new employee engagement and productivity, leading to faster integration into the company.

Challenge: **No business plan with clearly defined objectives**
Fraserism: Develop a comprehensive business plan with clearly defined objectives and strategies to achieve them. Regularly review and adjust the plan as necessary to ensure it remains relevant.
Potential Prompt: What steps can I take to develop a comprehensive business plan with defined objectives?
Benefit: A well-defined business plan with clear objectives helps ensure the company is headed in the right direction, improving overall efficiency, and increasing the likelihood of success.

Challenge: **No clearly defined job roles and KPIs**
Fraserism: Clearly define job roles and responsibilities, along with Key Performance Indicators (KPIs) to measure performance. Provide

regular feedback and support to employees to help them achieve their goals.

Potential Prompt: How can I create clear job roles and KPIs for my team?

Benefit: Clearly defined job roles and KPIs improve employee performance, which leads to increased productivity and higher quality work.

Challenge: **No Mission, Vision, and Values statement**

Fraserism: Develop a Mission, Vision, and Values statement that reflects the company's goals and values. Ensure all employees understand and are aligned with these statements.

Potential Prompt: How can I develop a Mission, Vision, and Values statement that accurately reflects my company?

Benefit: A well-defined Mission, Vision, and Values statement helps ensure all employees are working towards a common goal, improving overall productivity and employee engagement.

Challenge: **No regular team meetings or calls**

Fraserism: Schedule regular team meetings or calls to discuss current projects and any issues that may arise. Ensure all employees can provide input and feedback.

Potential Prompt: How often should I schedule team meetings to stay on top of current projects and issues?

Benefit: Regular team meetings or calls help ensure everyone is on the same page and any issues are addressed quickly, leading to increased productivity and a more efficient workflow.

Challenge: **No HR or personnel department to ensure compliance with employment laws.**

Fraserism: Consider creating an HR or personnel department to manage employee issues, ensure compliance with employment laws, and handle employee training and development.

Potential Prompt: What are the benefits of having an HR or personnel department in my company?

Benefit: Having an HR or personnel department helps ensure all employee-related issues are managed properly and in compliance with employment laws, reducing the risk of legal issues and increasing employee satisfaction.

Challenge: **Difficulty to stay motivated and achieve growth through meaningful work**

Fraserism: Clearly define personal goals for the year ahead, along with actionable steps to achieve them. Regularly review progress towards these goals and adjust, as necessary.

Potential Prompt: How can I define personal goals and create a meaningful work environment for myself and staff for the year ahead?

Benefit: Clearly defined personal goals help ensure personal growth and motivation, leading to increased productivity and each member enjoying meaningful work that keeps them on point, on form and on fire.

Challenge: **Allowing sales staff to make key decisions unsupervised**

Fraserism: Implement a system of checks and balances where sales staff can make certain decisions within their area of expertise, but these decisions must be reviewed and approved by a higher-up. This helps to ensure that decisions made align with the company's goals and are well thought-out.

Potential Prompt: "How can we empower our sales staff to make decisions while also ensuring that these decisions align with the company's goals?"

Benefit: By giving sales staff more autonomy in decision-making, you may increase their sense of ownership and engagement in their work, leading to higher motivation and productivity.

Challenge: **Sales staff may not feel incentivized to take on more responsibility**

Fraserism: Create a clear and transparent system for incentivizing and rewarding sales staff for taking on more responsibility, such as through promotions, bonuses, or other benefits. This can encourage staff to work harder and take on more challenging tasks.

Potential Prompt: "How can we incentivize our sales staff to take on more responsibility and grow within the company?"

Benefit: By incentivizing and rewarding sales staff for taking on more responsibility, you may increase their motivation to work harder and take on more challenging tasks, leading to improved performance and growth for the business.

Challenge: **Without regular training, sales staff may struggle to perform well**

Fraserism: Implement a regular training program for sales staff to keep them up to date on the latest industry trends and best practices. This can help them to stay motivated and engaged in their work, leading to improved performance and results.

Potential Prompt: "How can we ensure that our sales staff are regularly trained and up to date on the latest industry trends and best practices?"

Benefit: Regular training for sales staff can help to improve their performance, increase their motivation and engagement in their work, and lead to better results for the business.

Challenge: **Without effective delegation (or automation), leaders may become overwhelmed**

Fraserism: Learn to delegate tasks effectively by identifying the strengths and weaknesses of each team member, assigning tasks accordingly, and providing clear instructions and expectations. This can help leaders to free up their time to focus on high-level strategic goals.

Potential Prompt: "How can we improve our delegation skills to ensure that we are maximizing our time and resources?"

Benefit: Effective delegation can help leaders to free up their time and focus on high-level strategic goals, leading to improved performance and growth for the business.

Challenge: **No system in place for dealing with staff suggestions and complaints**

Fraserism: It is important to establish a system for handling staff suggestions and complaints. This can involve setting up a suggestion box, creating an online forum, or holding regular meetings to discuss concerns. It is also important to acknowledge and respond to all suggestions and complaints in a timely and respectful manner, and to follow up with staff to ensure their concerns have been addressed.

Potential Prompt: "What steps can I take to create a system for handling staff suggestions and complaints?"

Benefit: By implementing a system for handling staff suggestions and complaints, employees will feel heard, valued, and respected, leading to increased engagement, loyalty, and productivity.

Challenge: **Failing to thank staff personally or in company newsletters & emails**
Fraserism: It is important to regularly thank staff in company communications, such as newsletters, emails, or press releases. This can involve highlighting individual accomplishments or successes, sharing positive feedback from customers or clients, or recognizing team efforts. By publicly thanking staff, they will feel appreciated and motivated to continue working hard. Potential Prompt: "please create a sop detailing 10 different ways to thank staff for their effort, commitment and hard work."
Benefit: By publicly thanking staff in company communications, employees will feel valued and appreciated, leading to increased loyalty, job satisfaction, and productivity.

Challenge: **No loyalty program for staff and customers**
Fraserism: It is important to establish a loyalty program for both staff and customers. This can involve offering discounts, rewards, or special benefits for loyal employees or customers. By providing incentives for loyalty, employees will be motivated to continue working for your business, while customers will be motivated to continue purchasing from you. Potential Prompt: "please create an SOP detailing effective strategies for implementing a loyalty program for staff and customers."
Benefit: By implementing a loyalty program for staff and customers, you can increase retention rates, reduce turnover, and build a stronger brand reputation.

 Q. Are you leading and managing your staff effectively? Do you use AI to help you to better lead and manage your team? Do you use AI to help you gain clarity, vision, and purpose to embrace, create and live your vision?

1. Yes. All done, planned, documented & implemented in the business.

2. On the case. Working towards it, documenting it.

3. Oops. No, not yet completed (or started).

4. This is all too overwhelming. I Need help with this – fast.

Growth and Exit Strategy

It's essential for companies to have a plan in place for growth and eventual exit. A growth strategy is like a roadmap that outlines the steps a company will take to expand its reach and increase its profits. Just like a driver needs a map to reach their destination, a company needs a growth strategy to achieve its financial goals.

For example, a company may decide to expand into new markets or develop new products to attract more customers and generate more revenue. This is like a driver taking a detour to explore new roads and find a quicker route to their destination.

However, it's not enough to just have a growth strategy in place. It's also crucial to have an exit strategy that outlines how stakeholders can exit their investment in the company. This is like a traveler knowing how they will get back home after reaching their destination. An exit strategy ensures that stakeholders have a clear path to sell their shares, merge with another company, or be acquired by another business.

By having both a growth strategy and exit strategy in place, companies can provide stakeholders, shareholders, and investors with a sense of security and confidence in the future of the company. Just like a well-planned road trip with a clear destination and return route, having a growth and exit strategy ensures the long-term success and sustainability of a company.

Q. How and when do you plan to exit your business? ☐

Each of the points below are split into 4 parts.

- **Challenge:** common issue or obstacle often faced by business owners
- **Fraserism:** a helpful hint, tip, quote, or suggestion to help you in overcoming a challenge.

- **Potential Prompt:** a question, task, and prompt to ask your preferred ai-powered VA.
- **Benefit:** The potential benefit of researching, documenting, executing, automating, and refining a task, process, procedure, or workflow that addresses the underlying challenge.

Challenge: **No written business plan, customer journey, martech stack or marketing strategy**
Fraserism: I recommend developing a comprehensive business plan that outlines your company's objectives, strategies, and tactics. This plan should include a detailed analysis of your market, competition, and financial projections.
Potential Prompt: Can you guide me on how to create a comprehensive business plan that includes market analysis, competition analysis, and financial projections?
Benefit: Developing a written business plan can help you clarify your business goals, identify potential challenges and opportunities, and provide a roadmap for growth and success.

Challenge: **No written growth strategy**
Fraserism: I suggest developing a growth strategy that identifies opportunities for expansion, such as new markets, products or services, partnerships, or acquisitions.
Potential Prompt: How can I develop a growth strategy for my business that identifies new markets and revenue streams?
Benefit: Developing a written growth strategy can help you identify opportunities for expansion, allocate resources effectively, and stay competitive in your industry.

Challenge: **No written exit strategy**
Fraserism: I recommend developing an exit strategy that outlines your options for selling, merging, or transferring ownership of your business.
Potential Prompt: Can you help me create an exit strategy for my business that maximizes my return on investment?
Benefit: Developing a written exit strategy can help you maximize your return on investment, prepare for unforeseen circumstances, and ensure a smooth transition of ownership.

240

Challenge: **Not winning government contracts**
Fraserism: I suggest researching the requirements for local and central government contracts and ensuring that your business meets all necessary qualifications.
Potential Prompt: How can I ensure that my business meets the necessary qualifications to bid for local and central government contracts?
Benefit: Meeting the requirements for government contracts can help you access new business opportunities, diversify your revenue streams, and establish credibility in your industry.

Challenge: **Not meeting the requirements for larger private sector contracts**
Fraserism: I recommend researching the requirements for larger private sector contracts and ensuring that your business meets all necessary qualifications.
Potential Prompt: How can I ensure that my business meets the necessary qualifications to bid for larger private sector contracts?
Benefit: Meeting the requirements for larger private sector contracts can help you compete for high-value contracts, increase revenue, and establish credibility in your industry.

Challenge: **No protection against a legal dispute with staff,**
Fraserism: I suggest developing clear policies and procedures for addressing disputes with staff and ensuring that you have adequate insurance coverage.
Potential Prompt: How can I protect my business in the event of a legal dispute with staff?
Benefit: Having protection in the event of a legal dispute with staff can help you avoid costly legal fees, minimize damage to your reputation, and maintain positive relationships with your employees.

Challenge: **No SOPs or automated workflows, processes, or procedures in place**
Fraserism: I recommend delegating responsibilities to trusted employees and developing systems and procedures that enable your business to operate smoothly without your constant presence.
Potential Prompt: How can I ensure that my business can run day-to-day without me having to be there?

Benefit: Being able to run your business day-to-day without being there can help you scale your business, especially with clearly defined SOPs and automated workflows and processes in place.

Challenge: **Your stakeholders are not satisfied with the current level of sales and turnover.**
Fraserism: Conduct a market analysis to identify potential growth opportunities and develop a strategic growth plan. This plan should include identifying new markets, developing new products or services, and improving marketing and sales strategies.
Potential Prompt: What steps can I take to increase sales and turnover for my business?
Benefit: Developing a strategic growth plan can help increase sales and turnover, leading to increased profitability and market share.

Challenge: **You and your stakeholders are not satisfied with the current level of profitability.**
Fraserism: Conduct a financial analysis to identify areas where costs can be reduced, and revenue can be increased. This may include streamlining operations, renegotiating contracts with suppliers, and improving pricing strategies.
Potential Prompt: How can I increase profitability for my business?
Benefit: Improving profitability can provide the business with more resources to invest in growth and expansion, as well as increasing returns for shareholders and stakeholders.

Challenge: **You and your stakeholders are not satisfied with the current level of market share.**
Fraserism: Conduct a competitive analysis to identify areas where the business can differentiate itself and gain market share. This may include improving product quality, enhancing customer service, and expanding distribution channels.
Potential Prompt: What steps can I take to increase market share for my business?
Benefit: Increasing market share can lead to increased brand recognition, revenue, and profitability.

Challenge: **You are not satisfied with the number of product lines you have.**

Fraserism: Conduct a product analysis to identify potential new product lines that align with the business's core competencies and market demand.

Potential Prompt: How can I expand my product lines to better serve my customers?

Benefit: Expanding product lines can provide new revenue streams and opportunities for growth.

Challenge: **Not disruptive in your marketplace.**

Fraserism: Conduct a market analysis to identify areas where the business can innovate and differentiate itself from competitors. This may include introducing new technologies, improving customer experience, or developing unique marketing strategies.

Potential Prompt: What can I do to disrupt my marketplace and stand out from competitors?

Benefit: Being disruptive can lead to increased market share, profitability, and brand recognition.

Challenge: **Customer service & support infrastructure cannot cope with a 30% growth.**

Fraserism: Develop and implement a customer service plan that includes hiring additional staff, improving communication channels, and providing additional training for existing staff.

Potential Prompt: How can I ensure that my customer service infrastructure can manage significant growth?

Benefit: Providing quality customer service can lead to increased customer loyalty and positive word-of-mouth marketing.

Challenge: **You require more or new funding or investment**

Fraserism: Develop a funding plan that includes identifying potential sources of funding, such as investors, grants, or loans, and creating a detailed financial plan that shows potential returns on investment.

Potential Prompt: How can I obtain the funding I need to grow my business?

Benefit: Securing funding can provide the resources needed to invest in growth and expansion.

Challenge: **You do not have a repayment plan or ROI plan in place.**

Fraserism: Develop a financial plan that includes a repayment plan and ROI projections to provide investors with a clear understanding of potential returns on investment.

Potential Prompt: How can I create a repayment plan and ROI plan to attract potential investors?

Benefit: Having a clear repayment plan and ROI projections can make the business more attractive to potential investors, increasing the likelihood of securing funding.

Q. Do you have a clear growth plan and exit strategy in place? Do you use AI to help you to better scale and manage your growth? Do you use AI to help you gain clarity, vision, and purpose to embrace, create and live your vision?

1. Yes. All done, planned, documented & implemented in the business.

2. On the case. Working towards it, documenting it.

3. Oops. No, not yet completed (or started).

4. This is all too overwhelming. I Need help with this – fast.

Quality Management System

Having a quality management system (QMS) in place is crucial for businesses that want to join approved supplier lists or tender for government contracts. The complexity lies in the requirements and standards that need to be met to be considered for these opportunities. The importance of a QMS lies in the many benefits it can bring to a business, such as increased efficiency, improved customer satisfaction, and a better overall reputation.

To meet the requirements of government contracts and approved supplier lists, businesses need to demonstrate that they have effective quality management systems in place. This means having documented policies and procedures that ensure that products or services are consistent and of a high quality, as well as a process for continuous improvement. Without a QMS, a business may struggle to meet the necessary standards and requirements, which can result in lost opportunities and damage to their reputation.

ISO (International Organization for Standardization) offers a range of globally recognized standards that businesses can use to establish frameworks for quality, safety, and environmental management. There are various ISO standards, such as ISO 9001 for quality management, ISO 14001 for environmental management, and ISO 27001 for information security management.

In addition, ISO standards can help businesses to comply with regulatory requirements and demonstrate a commitment to quality, safety, and environmental responsibility, which can help to build trust and establish strong relationships with customers and partners. ISO standards are also adaptable to various industries, making them a useful tool for businesses of all sizes and types, from startups to multinational corporations. Overall, implementing ISO standards can provide a range of advantages for businesses, including improving operational efficiency, increasing customer satisfaction, reducing risk, meeting regulatory requirements, and enhancing reputation. As such, businesses that implement ISO standards are better positioned to achieve sustainable growth and long-term success.

However, having a QMS is not just important for compliance purposes. It can also bring a range of benefits to a business. For example, a QMS can help to increase efficiency by identifying and eliminating unnecessary steps in a process, reducing waste, and improving productivity. It can also help to improve customer satisfaction by ensuring that products or services meet or exceed their expectations. Additionally, having a QMS can enhance a business's reputation, making them more attractive to potential customers and partners.

So, the importance of having a quality management system in place for businesses cannot be overstated, especially when seeking to join approved supplier lists or if you plan tendering for government contracts. The complexity of the requirements and standards, coupled with the benefits that a QMS can bring, make it an essential component of a serious growth strategy.

Q. Do you have a quality management system in place? ☐

Each of the points below are split into 4 parts.

- **Challenge:** common issue or obstacle often faced by business owners
- **Fraserism:** a helpful hint, tip, quote, or suggestion to help you in overcoming a challenge.
- **Potential Prompt:** a question, task, and prompt to ask your preferred ai-powered VA.
- **Benefit:** The potential benefit of researching, documenting, executing, automating, and refining a task, process, procedure, or workflow that addresses the underlying challenge.

Challenge: **Not knowing the 8 Quality Management principles.**
Fraserism: The 8 Quality Management principles are Customer Focus, Leadership, Engagement of People, Process Approach, Improvement, Evidence-based Decision Making, Relationship

Management, and Continual Improvement.
Potential Prompt: "Can you explain the 8 Quality Management principles?"

Benefit: Understanding the 8 Quality Management principles is crucial for developing an effective Quality Management System. This knowledge helps businesses to better serve their customers, continuously improve their processes, and achieve their goals.

Challenge: **Lack of motivation and commitment to applying Quality Management principles.**
Fraserism: It is important to be motivated and committed to applying the 8 Quality Management principles in your business. This can be achieved by ensuring that all staff understand the principles, their role in implementing them, and the benefits they provide.
Potential Prompt: "How can I motivate my staff to apply the 8 Quality Management principles in our business?"

Benefit: Motivated and committed staff can help to create a culture of quality within the business, leading to improved customer satisfaction, higher quality products or services, and increased efficiency.

Challenge: **Not having a written quality policy for your business.**
Fraserism: A written quality policy is essential for communicating your commitment to quality to both staff and customers. It should be a clear and concise statement of your business's commitment to meeting customer requirements and continuously improving.
Potential Prompt: "How can I create a quality policy for my business?"

Benefit: A written quality policy provides a clear direction for the business and helps to ensure that all staff are working towards the same goals. It can also be used to demonstrate compliance with relevant standards and regulations.

Challenge: **Inadequate allocation of human, technical & financial resources to your QMS.**
Fraserism: Adequate allocation of resources is essential for the

successful implementation of a Quality Management System. This includes allocating appropriate human resources, providing access to technical resources, and allocating sufficient financial resources.

Potential Prompt: "How can I ensure that my business has allocated appropriate resources for our QMS?"

Benefit: Adequate resource allocation can help to ensure that the QMS is effectively implemented and maintained, leading to improved quality, increased efficiency, and improved customer satisfaction.

Challenge: **Not identifying a certification body for final assessment.**

Fraserism: It is important to identify a certification body for final assessment early in the QMS implementation process. This can help to ensure that the QMS is designed to meet the requirements of the chosen standard and can help to avoid any last-minute surprises.

Potential Prompt: "How can I choose a certification body for our QMS assessment?"

Benefit: Choosing a certification body early in the process can help to ensure that the QMS is effectively implemented and maintained, leading to successful certification and improved business performance.

Challenge: **Not conducting a GAP Analysis & Management Review of the business.**

Fraserism: Conducting a GAP Analysis and Management Review is essential for identifying areas where the business does not meet the requirements of the chosen standard. This information can then be used to develop a plan for addressing these gaps.

Potential Prompt: "How can I conduct a GAP Analysis & Management Review of my business?"

Benefit: Conducting a GAP Analysis and Management Review can help to identify areas for improvement and ensure that the QMS is effectively implemented and maintained.

Challenge: Without a schedule for internal audits, it is difficult to

248

ensure that the QMS is working correctly.

Fraserism: Create a schedule for regular internal audits of your QMS to identify any issues that may need to be addressed. Assign the appropriate resources to conduct these audits and ensure that they are conducted in a timely manner.

Potential Prompt: Can you describe your current process for scheduling and conducting internal audits of your QMS?

Benefit: Regular internal audits can help identify potential issues before they become major problems and can ensure that your QMS is working as intended.

Challenge: **Internal auditing does not add value to the business**

Fraserism: Ensure that your internal auditing process is designed to add value to the business and assist management in identifying areas for improvement. This can be achieved by using the findings from internal audits to drive continuous improvement.

Potential Prompt: How do you ensure that your internal auditing process adds value to the business and assists management in identifying areas for improvement?

Benefit: A well-designed internal auditing process can help drive continuous improvement, increase efficiency, and reduce costs.

Challenge: **No developed SOPs or written instructions**

Fraserism: Develop procedures and written instructions for all aspects of your business to ensure consistent and reliable processes. Make sure that these procedures and instructions are easily accessible to all employees.

Potential Prompt: Can you describe the process for developing procedures and written instructions for your business?

Benefit: Well-developed procedures and written instructions can help ensure consistent and reliable processes, reduce errors, and improve efficiency.

Challenge: **Not Conducting regular management reviews of your QMS**

Fraserism: Schedule regular management reviews of your QMS to ensure that it continues to meet your business objectives. Use these reviews to identify areas for improvement and take action to address any issues.

Potential Prompt: Can you describe how you conduct regular management reviews of your QMS?

Benefit: Regular management reviews can help ensure that your QMS continues to meet your business objectives and identify areas for improvement.

Challenge: **Internal auditors auditing their own department or work area**

Fraserism: Ensure that your internal auditors do not audit their own department or work area. Assign auditors from other departments or consider hiring external auditors to conduct these audits.

Potential Prompt: Can you describe your process for selecting and assigning internal auditors to conduct audits?

Benefit: Objectivity and avoidance of conflicts of interest can help ensure the integrity of the internal audit process and identify potential issues that may have been overlooked.

Q. Do you have a QMS strategy in place? Do you use AI to help you to better manage Quality in your business? Do you use AI to help you gain clarity, vision, and purpose to embrace, create and live your vision?

1. Yes. All done, planned, documented & implemented in the business.
2. On the case. Working towards it, documenting it.
3. Oops. No, not yet completed (or started).
4. This is all too overwhelming. I Need help with this – fast.

Corporate Social Responsibility

Corporate Social Responsibility (CSR) is an approach taken by businesses to operate in a way that benefits society, the environment, and the economy, beyond their legal obligations. A well-designed CSR strategy can be a powerful tool for businesses to differentiate themselves from their competitors and enhance their reputation.

Think of it like building a house. The foundation of the house is built on the legal requirements that businesses must comply with, but the CSR strategy is like the roof that provides an additional layer of protection and support. By implementing a CSR strategy, businesses can attract socially conscious consumers who want to support brands that align with their values, and this can help to build a strong brand image and reputation.

In addition, implementing a CSR strategy can help businesses to attract and retain talented employees who are passionate about making a positive impact on society and the environment. Just like how a house needs a strong support system to keep it standing, a business needs a team of motivated employees to keep it thriving. By providing employees with a sense of purpose and pride in their work through CSR initiatives, businesses can improve employee morale and motivation.

Finally, implementing a CSR strategy can have a positive impact on a business's financial performance. Just like how a well-built house can withstand different weather conditions and provide comfort and protection, a CSR strategy can help businesses to reduce costs, enhance their reputation, and improve relationships with stakeholders. This can lead to increased revenue and profits, making it a smart investment for businesses.

Implementing a CSR strategy is a win-win for businesses and society. It can help businesses build a strong brand image, attract, and retain employees, and improve financial performance, while also contributing to a more sustainable and responsible society.

Q. What issues and causes are your customers concerned about?

☐

Each of the points below are split into 4 parts.

- **Challenge:** common issue or obstacle often faced by business owners
- **Fraserism:** a helpful hint, tip, quote, or suggestion to help you in overcoming a challenge.
- **Potential Prompt:** a question, task, and prompt to ask your preferred ai-powered VA.
- **Benefit:** The potential benefit of researching, documenting, executing, automating, and refining a task, process, procedure, or workflow that addresses the underlying challenge.

Challenge: **Not having a documented and implemented CSR strategy**
Fraserism: Create a comprehensive CSR strategy that outlines your goals, initiatives, and metrics for success. This will help ensure that your business is able to reap the benefits of CSR.
Potential Prompt: What steps can I take to develop a comprehensive CSR strategy for my business?
Benefit: By creating a comprehensive CSR strategy, your business can improve its reputation and attract more socially conscious customers, leading to increased revenue and profits.

Challenge: **Without a CSR strategy, your brand image and reputation may suffer**
Fraserism: Incorporate CSR initiatives into your business practices and communicate these efforts to your stakeholders through various channels such as social media, press releases, and sustainability reports.
Potential Prompt: How can I communicate my business's CSR initiatives to my stakeholders effectively?
Benefit: By enhancing your brand image and reputation through CSR, your business can differentiate itself from competitors and attract socially conscious customers and talented employees.

Challenge: **Not leveraging the impact that CSR can have on customer loyalty and retention.**
Fraserism: Implement CSR initiatives that align with your customers' values and communicate the positive impact of these efforts to your customers.
Potential Prompt: How can I align my business's CSR initiatives with my customers' values?
Benefit: By improving customer loyalty and retention through CSR, your business can increase revenue and profits eventually.

Challenge: **Your business may struggle to differentiate itself from competitors**
Fraserism: Incorporate unique CSR initiatives that align with your business's values and mission and communicate the positive impact of these initiatives to your stakeholders.
Potential Prompt: How can I differentiate my business from competitors through CSR initiatives?
Benefit: By standing out from competitors through CSR, your business can attract socially conscious customers and talented employees.

Challenge: **Your business may miss attracting socially conscious consumers.**
Fraserism: Implement CSR initiatives that align with your target customers' values and communicate the positive impact of these efforts through various channels.
Potential Prompt: How can I attract socially conscious consumers through CSR initiatives?
Benefit: By attracting socially conscious customers through CSR, your business can increase revenue and profits eventually.

Challenge: **Your business may struggle to attract and retain talented employees**
Fraserism: Incorporate CSR initiatives into your company culture and communicate the positive impact of these efforts to current and potential employees.
Potential Prompt: How can I attract and retain talented employees through CSR initiatives?
Benefit: By attracting and retaining talented employees who

prioritize social responsibility, your business can improve operational efficiency and increase revenue and profits.

Challenge: **Your business may struggle to improve employee morale and motivation.**
Fraserism: Implement CSR initiatives that align with your employees' values and involve employees in the development and execution of these initiatives.
Potential Prompt: How can I improve employee morale and motivation through CSR initiatives?
Benefit: By improving employee morale and motivation through CSR, your business can increase productivity and efficiency, leading to increased revenue and profits.

Challenge: **How can you ensure that your CSR strategy aligns with the relevant legislation?**
Fraserism: Research the applicable legislation in your jurisdiction and consult with legal experts to ensure your CSR strategy aligns with all relevant requirements. Review your strategy regularly to ensure ongoing compliance with any updates or changes in legislation.
Potential Prompt: "What steps can I take to ensure that my CSR strategy aligns with all applicable legislation in my jurisdiction?"
Benefit: Ensuring legal compliance can help protect your business from potential legal and reputational risks.

Challenge: **Confirming the potential consequences of not complying with CSR legislation**
Fraserism: Failure to comply with CSR legislation can result in legal penalties, fines, and damage to your business's reputation. Develop and implement a comprehensive CSR strategy that complies with all applicable legislation to mitigate these risks.
Potential Prompt: "What are the potential consequences if my business fails to comply with CSR legislation in our jurisdiction?"
Benefit: Understanding the potential consequences can motivate you to take the necessary steps to ensure legal compliance.

Challenge: **How often to review a CSR strategy to ensure ongoing compliance**

Fraserism: Review your CSR strategy regularly, at least annually, to ensure ongoing compliance with relevant legislation. Keep up to date with any changes or updates to legislation and adjust your strategy accordingly.

Potential Prompt: "How often should I review and update my business's CSR strategy to ensure legal compliance?"

Benefit: Regular reviews can help you stay current with any changes or updates to legislation and mitigate any potential legal or reputational risks.

Challenge: **How can you ensure that your CSR strategy meets stakeholder expectations**

Fraserism: Consult with stakeholders, including employees, customers, suppliers, and community members, to understand their expectations of your business's CSR practices. Incorporate this feedback into your strategy while also ensuring compliance with all relevant legislation.

Potential Prompt: "How can I ensure that my business's CSR strategy aligns with stakeholder expectations while also meeting all legal requirements?"

Benefit: Aligning your CSR strategy with stakeholder expectations can improve your business's reputation and build trust with your stakeholders.

Challenge: **How to implement effective CSR practices in your business**

Fraserism: Develop a comprehensive CSR strategy that includes measurable goals, targets, and action plans. Train employees on CSR practices and integrate CSR considerations into all business operations and decision-making processes.

Potential Prompt: "What are some steps my business can take to effectively implement CSR practices?"

Benefit: Implementing effective CSR practices can improve your business's reputation, attract customers and employees, and drive long-term success.

Challenge: **How to ensure that all employees are aware of the CSR policies and procedures**

Fraserism: Develop and implement an effective training program to educate all employees on the company's CSR policies and procedures. Regularly communicate updates and changes to ensure ongoing awareness and compliance.

Potential Prompt: "How can I ensure that all employees in my business are aware of our CSR policies and procedures?"

Benefit: Educating employees on CSR policies and procedures can help ensure legal compliance and improve the effectiveness of your CSR practices.

Challenge: **How to integrate CSR considerations into your decision-making processes**

Fraserism: Develop a comprehensive CSR strategy that includes measurable goals and targets and integrate CSR considerations into all business operations and decision-making processes. Train employees in CSR practices and establish clear accountability and reporting procedures.

Potential Prompt: "How can I integrate CSR considerations into my business operations and decision-making processes?"

Benefit: Integrating CSR considerations can improve your business's reputation, reduce risk, and drive long-term success.

Q. Do you have a CSR strategy in place? Do you use AI to help you to better manage your Corporate Social Responsibilities? Do you use AI to help you gain clarity, vision, and purpose to embrace, create and live your vision?

1. Yes. All done, planned, documented & implemented in the business.

2. On the case. Working towards it, documenting it.

3. Oops. No, not yet completed (or started).

4. This is all too overwhelming. I Need help with this – fast.

Franchising & Licensing

Expanding your business is a smart move for any entrepreneur looking to increase revenue and reach new markets. Franchising and licensing are two effective ways to achieve this goal. Franchising means allowing someone to use your entire business model, including your products or services, brand, and other proprietary information. Licensing, on the other hand, involves granting someone the right to use your intellectual property, such as patents, trademarks, and copyrights, in exchange for a fee.

By franchising or licensing your business, you can capitalize on the knowledge and resources of others to scale your business faster than if you were to do it alone. You can also generate extra income streams by charging franchise fees or licensing royalties. Moreover, by allowing others to use your brand and intellectual property, you can expand your business's visibility and reputation.

Nevertheless, franchising and licensing come with certain risks and challenges. For instance, you must make sure that your franchisees or licensees adhere to your business's values and standards. You must also negotiate and prepare franchise and licensing agreements carefully to safeguard your intellectual property and limit your exposure to liability.

In conclusion, franchising and licensing are powerful tools for expanding your business and optimizing revenue streams. However, to make it a success, you should plan carefully, consult professionals for legal and financial advice, and manage your franchisees or licensees efficiently. By doing so, you can leverage these models to take your business to the next level.

Q. What IP could you license or franchise on a per country basis? ☐

Each of the points below are split into 4 parts.

- **Challenge:** common issue or obstacle often faced by business owners
- **Fraserism:** a helpful hint, tip, quote, or suggestion to help you in overcoming a challenge.
- **Potential Prompt:** a question, task, and prompt to ask your preferred ai-powered VA.
- **Benefit:** The potential benefit of researching, documenting, executing, automating, and refining a task, process, procedure, or workflow that addresses the underlying challenge.

Challenge: **Not having a clear idea of the ideal Licensee or Franchise for the business.**
Fraserism: Define the characteristics and qualifications of the ideal Licensee or Franchise by conducting market research, analyzing industry trends, and evaluating the needs of the business. Create a comprehensive profile that includes traits such as experience, education, financial capability, and personality traits.
Potential Prompt: What steps can I take to define the ideal Licensee or Franchise for my business?
Benefit: By defining the ideal Licensee or Franchisee, the business owner can better identify and attract suitable candidates, increasing the chances of success.

Challenge: **Not deciding on the investment required for the "opportunity".**
Fraserism: Conduct a thorough analysis of the costs associated with the business, including fees, equipment, and training expenses, to determine the initial investment required from the Licensee or Franchise. Consider the market demand, competition, and potential profitability when setting the investment amount.
Potential Prompt: How can I determine the initial investment required for my Licensee/Franchise opportunity?
Benefit: By determining the required investment, the business owner can set realistic expectations and attract Licensees/Franchisees who are financially capable of investing in the business.

Challenge: **Unclear basis for determining a Territory.**
Fraserism: Conduct market research to determine the most suitable territories for the business, based on factors such as market demand, competition, and demographic characteristics. Consider creating a territory map that clearly outlines the boundaries of each area.
Potential Prompt: What are the steps to determine the suitable territories for my business?
Benefit: By establishing clear territories, the business owner can avoid disputes among Licensees/Franchises and ensure efficient allocation of resources.

Challenge: **Unclear on the number of suspects in each territory.**
Fraserism: Conduct market research to determine the number of potential customers in each territory. Consider factors such as population density, income levels, and consumer behavior.
Potential Prompt: How can I determine the number of suspects in each territory?
Benefit: By understanding the potential customer base in each territory, the business owner can develop targeted marketing strategies and set realistic revenue expectations.

Challenge: **Unclear on the value of each territory.**
Fraserism: Evaluate the market demand, competition, and potential profitability of each territory to determine its value. Consider factors such as population density, consumer behavior, and the presence of competitors.
Potential Prompt: How can I determine the value of each territory?
Benefit: By understanding the value of each territory, the business owner can allocate resources effectively and set realistic revenue expectations.

Challenge: **No Launch plan for each territory.**
Fraserism: Develop a comprehensive Launch plan for each territory that includes marketing strategies, sales tactics, and operational procedures. Consider factors such as local regulations, market demand, and competition.
Potential Prompt: What are the essential elements of a Launch plan for a new territory?
Benefit: By having a Launch plan in place, the business owner can

ensure a smooth and successful launch of the business in each new territory.

Challenge: **No License/Franchise Agreement or "Information Memorandum" in place.**
Fraserism: Engage legal counsel to draft a comprehensive License/Franchise Agreement that clearly outlines the rights and responsibilities of both parties. Consider factors such as term length, fees, royalties, and intellectual property rights.
Potential Prompt: What are the essential elements of a License or Franchise Agreement?
Benefit: By having a clear and comprehensive License/Franchise Agreement, the business owner can protect their intellectual property and avoid legal disputes.

Challenge: **Not having protected IPR can lead to potential legal issues and loss of revenue.**
Fraserism: It is important to register trademarks, patents, and copyrights to protect IPR. Seek legal advice to determine the appropriate steps needed to protect your intellectual property.
Potential Prompt: What are the steps needed to register a trademark and protect my intellectual property?
Benefit: Protecting IPR can prevent others from copying your products or services and can create a competitive advantage.

Challenge: **Not having determined what IPR a franchisee will receive can lead to misunderstandings and disputes.**
Fraserism: Clearly outline in the franchise agreement what IPR the franchisee will receive for their investment. This can include trademark usage, proprietary software, and other intellectual property.
Potential Prompt: What intellectual property will a franchisee receive for their investment in my business?
Benefit: Clearly outlining what IPR a franchisee will receive can help prevent disputes and create a more productive and profitable franchise relationship.

Challenge: **Not having a plan for replacing a franchise in a territory**

260

Fraserism: Have a plan in place for replacing a franchise in a territory. This can include identifying potential replacement candidates and providing support to ensure a smooth transition.

Potential Prompt: What steps should I take to replace a franchise in a territory if necessary?

Benefit: Having a replacement plan can help ensure continuity of operations and customer loyalty in the event of a franchisee leaving the business.

Challenge: **Not being featured in press or trade journals**

Fraserism: Develop relationships with journalists and editors to secure coverage in local, national, and international press and trade journals/magazines. Share newsworthy developments and unique perspectives to increase the chances of being featured.

Potential Prompt: How can I get my business featured in trade journals and online publications?

Benefit: Being featured in press and trade journals can increase brand awareness, credibility, and potential customer base.

Challenge: **Not completing a competitor analysis can lead to missed opportunities**

Fraserism: Conduct a comprehensive competitor analysis to understand the strengths and weaknesses of competitors, identify gaps in the market, and develop strategies for differentiation.

Potential Prompt: What is involved in a comprehensive competitor analysis?

Benefit: Conducting a competitor analysis can provide valuable insights into the market, inform business strategy, and lead to increased competitiveness.

Challenge: **Not creating a marketing training program**

Fraserism: Develop a marketing training program for franchisees that includes messaging, branding, and marketing strategies. Provide ongoing support to ensure consistent and effective marketing across all territories.

Potential Prompt: How can I develop a marketing training program for franchisees?

Benefit: Creating a marketing training program can help ensure consistent and effective marketing across all territories, leading to increased revenue and profitability.

Challenge: **Not having a corporate franchisor website**
Fraserism: Develop a corporate franchisor website that highlights the brand, mission, and values. Provide franchisees with website templates that maintain consistency in branding and messaging.
Potential Prompt: How can I develop a corporate franchisor website and franchise websites?
Benefit: Having a strong online presence can increase brand awareness and credibility and provide potential customers with easy access to information about the franchise.

 Q. Are you considering franchising or licensing your intellectual property? Do you use AI to help you to better manage your franchise opportunity? Do you use AI to help you gain clarity, vision, and purpose to embrace, create and live your vision?

1. Yes. All done, planned, documented & implemented in the business.

2. On the case. Working towards it, documenting it.

3. Oops. No, not yet completed (or started).

4. This is all too overwhelming. I Need help with this – fast.

Compaq was a major computer hardware manufacturer with a peak revenue of $37 billion in 1997 and over 17,000 employees. However, Compaq failed to keep up with the rise of portable computing devices and the shift towards mobile technology.

Competitors like Dell and Apple were able to offer more innovative products and capture a larger share of the market. Compaq was eventually acquired by Hewlett-Packard in 2002, and its brand was phased out.

Get AI-powered help to save time, money & stress to do the jobs you hate, don't have time for, or simply don't want to do.

Reduce costs, improve efficiency & ROI to achieve your goals & objectives. It's your business. you're in control.
You make the decisions.
You decide what you want to achieve next.

About The Author

Fraser Hay is a seasoned business coach, consultant, and keynote speaker, recognised for his multi-award-winning entrepreneurship and global impact. Having delivered inspiring keynotes on **4** continents and authored over **20+** books available on Amazon, Fraser is dedicated to empowering individuals, managers, and founders to conquer personal, professional, and commercial challenges at every stage of their entrepreneurial journey.

With an innovative approach to coaching, consultancy, and technology solutions, Fraser helps individuals and entrepreneurs realise their vision without struggle, limitation, or fear. Drawing from his experience, Fraser has identified and tackled over 2000 common issues, challenges, and obstacles encountered in the entrepreneurial landscape.

Unlike traditional coaches, Fraser's methodology is grounded in practical solutions, documented insights, and guaranteed progress. Through webinars, keynote speeches, workshops, and coaching programs, he shares his wealth of knowledge and expertise to facilitate transformative growth for his clients.

As a TEDx keynote speaker with two decades of remote working experience, Fraser is committed to supporting owners, founders, and senior management teams in achieving their marketing objectives. He provides clarity, purpose, and measurable results, ensuring progress at every stage of the entrepreneurial journey.

Fraser's insightful quotes, or "Fraserisms," such as *"remember, life is happening for you, not to you."* serve as a mental espresso offering perspective and guidance to navigate life's challenges effectively.

Over the past **3** decades, Fraser has assisted entrepreneurs, managers, and business owners in over 40 countries, spanning various industries and business stages. His services encompass strategic planning, marketing automation, accountability coaching, and keynote presentations at prestigious conferences and conventions worldwide. He also accepts a limited number of 1-2-1 coaching clients per annum.

NEXT STEPS? Schedule a FREE Strategy Call via his website or if you can't wait, call him on +44 (0) 1542 663491.

FREE BONUS

As promised, if you're serious about embracing AI to create and live your vision and to automate the jobs you hate, don't have time and don't want to do, then you may find the following FREE resources on my website useful:

Both are available on my website at www.itstacksup.com

These webinars are practical, insightful and will help you to consider elements of your future business and marketing that you may not have thought of yet. They are fun, educational and will also challenge your thinking and existing assumptions to ensure that you get on point, on form and on fire.

Both are available on my website at www.itstacksup.com

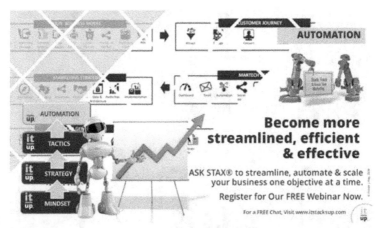

Sign up for our FREE Webinars before your competitors do.

Other Work by the Author

For more, visit: www.fraserhay.com

www.ingramcontent.com/pod-product-compliance
Lightning Source LLC
LaVergne TN
LVHW051439050326
832903LV00030BD/3167